TUESDAY @ TWELVE

Uncover Your Team's Natural Talent and

Dare to Achieve Greatness

Ian Kinnery

IAN KINNERY

Copyright © 2018 Ian Kinnery.

All rights reserved. No part of this publication may be reproduced, distributed, or transmitted in any form or by any means, including photocopying, recording, or other electronic or mechanical methods, without the prior written permission of the publisher, except in the case of brief quotations embodied in critical reviews and certain other noncommercial uses permitted by copyright law. For permission requests, write to the publisher, addressed "Attention: Permissions Coordinator," at the address below.

ISBN-13: 978-17 26327213

Any references to historical events, real people, or real places are used fictitiously. Names, characters, and places are products of the author's imagination.

Front cover image by Chemistry Marketing.

Published by Team Massive Results in the United Kingdom.

First edition 2018.

Team Massive Results,

Office 11 and 12

Beaumont House

74-76 Church Road

Stockton-on-Tees

TS18 1TW

www.teammassiveresults.com

ACKNOWLEDGEMENTS

This book has been written as a fable to try to communicate some of the lessons that I have learned on my journey and that I try to teach as a professional business coach. So, I really should mention everyone who has influenced me to date. But that would be an impossible task.

I have been blessed to have worked for and with some inspiring people in some exceptional businesses and also to have experienced the polar opposite. I am sure that I myself have represented both sides of the divide as a business owner and a business leader at various times.

I couldn't have produced this book without all of the people who have shown me 'stuff what works' over the years nor all of those people who have demonstrated 'what not to do', either. I won't mention them by name.

I would especially like to thank all of the clients and client companies that I have had the honour and pleasure to serve over the last twelve years as a business coach. They say that "when one teaches, two learn", and I have learned an enormous amount from my clients for which I shall ever be indebted to them.

The fable is based on the impact of the meeting rhythm as proposed by Verne Harnish and the team of Gazelles International Coaches, who are an exceptional bunch of people developing an awesome methodology for scaling up businesses. A lot of their principles are based on the work of great 'thought leaders' in the world of business and the wisdom freely expressed in their books and presentations which has been foundational in my personal growth. How I wish that I had started this journey of self-development with so much intention earlier in my life. As one of my coaches says, 'We don't know what we don't know and it's what we don't know that costs us'.

Finally, I would like to thank Hazel Raffle, my business manager here at Team Massive Results who makes doing what we do so much fun, along with our extended team including Joanna Collie, Anth Quinn and Matt McGough, and of course my family: Jayne Folkes, Emily Folkes and my two special canine collaborators Alfie and Buster who try to keep me sane, grounded and together.

IAN KINNERY

Dedicated to all the individuals who ever came together to form a winning team.

FOREWORD

'Scaling up' a business is challenging on many fronts. As a certified Gazelles coach, I help my clients and their teams tackle the four decision groups of 'People', 'Strategy', 'Execution' and 'Cash' that they have to get right in order to drive growth.

It strikes me that there is one major area of the 'People' decision (a whole series of both decisions and disciplines) that can either confound the entrepreneur that would scale up or indeed help him to scale quickly and effectively: that is the area of 'team' - more specifically, the leadership team.

In the growth journey of most businesses there seems to be a pivotal point where the thrusting entrepreneur can no longer grow the business on his own by the force of his own personality, skills and enthusiasm. There comes a time when he has to enrol and enlist a Senior Leadership Team.

Very often, what gets you here won't get you there. This becomes a dangerous place for founder-led businesses because the leader may have never experienced or been a part of a successful

Senior Leadership Team. Therefore, he has little or no idea how to create one or, indeed, how to lead one. The techniques and tactics that worked so well before we needed to lead leaders no longer work and frustration and tension grow on all parts.

Pat Lencioni once wrote that "if you could get all the people in the organisation rowing in the same direction, you could dominate any industry, in any market, against any competition, at any time" (Patrick M. Lencioni, "The Five Dysfunctions of a Team: A Leadership Fable", JOHN WILEY & SONS, 2002). Failure to develop a cohesive leadership team becomes a massive obstacle to successfully scaling up a business.

But it is more than that. Any business is both a reflection and an amplifier of what happens at the top of the organisation. If the top of the organisation is dysfunctional, that level of dysfunction will be magnified as we move further down through the business. If the leadership team is not really working as a team, the same will be true for all other levels of the organisation. It's therefore vitally important that we get the Senior Leadership Team right, with not only the right people in the right seats but also managed, motivated and led in the most appropriate and effective way.

The biggest lever we have to manage and motivate the Senior Leadership Team lies in the 'meeting rhythm' best described in 'scaling up'. If it is an intellectual challenge, sometimes our understanding the importance of engaging the people that work in our business is a comparatively small one next to the challenge of our developing the skills and the techniques necessary to deliver a team that is engaged and pulling in the same direction. This is definitely an area where there is a massive potential gap between 'knowing' and 'doing'.

The purpose of this book is to show how effective a team can be when its members get on the same page and start pulling in the same direction. It is designed to give an insight into the benefits of helping the leadership team to become a cohesive, focused unit and to give a case study of how it might be achieved. Those benefits are much more than just financial. Typically, team members start to have more fun, enjoy things more while performing both individually and collectively at a higher level.

It is not written as a 'how to' book: there is as much art as there is science in one's successfully leading a winning team and helping everyone to feel like a valued member of that team. You must find your own individual way of achieving this, in your own way, or keep on trying. I can't tell you how to do it. It will depend on your own profile and the interplay between all of the characters that make up the team. It is a very dynamic situation.

The book is fictional but the scenarios are based on real events with real people. The improvements are also real. A great leader can help a previously dysfunctional team to perform well. I hope to lift the veil on ways that even the most novice leader can start to make big changes quite easily.

You will see references to some universally applicable tools as you read the book; things like the 'meeting rhythm', which sets the heartbeat of the organisation, the 'WWW' ('Who, What, When') which brings a closed loop of accountability and the use of the numbers to direct the focus and attention of the team. As R.

Buckminster Fuller said, "If you want to teach people a new way of thinking, don't bother trying to teach them. Instead, give them a tool, the use of which will lead to new ways of thinking."

I commend intelligent use of these tools as you strive to turn your leadership team into a cohesive one. A team in which every member feels valued and proud to be a part, performing at a higher level as a consequence both individually and collectively. Ultimately, the role of the business leader is to grow the leaders within the business.

Myles Downey defines coaching, which is part of the leader's role, as "the series of conversations that help a person perform closer to his potential, understand his role or task, learn what he needs to learn in order to complete his role or task successfully, develop the skills required for the next role, and, on a good day, achieve fulfilment - and maybe a little joy- at work" (Myles Downey, "Effective Modern Coaching", LID PUBLISHING, 2014)

And that really is the desired outcomes for this book. To help you create fulfilment and a little joy at work. That way, you can positively impact every life that you touch.

CONTENTS

ACKNOWLEDGEMENTS .... - 3 -
FOREWORD .... - 6 -
CONTENTS .... - 10 -
PROLOGUE .... - 12 -
PART 1 .... - 14 -
INTRODUCTION .... - 15 -
   CHAPTER 1 .... - 18 -
   CHAPTER 2 .... - 26 -
   CHAPTER 3 .... - 34 -
   CHAPTER 4 .... - 38 -
PART 2 .... - 44 -
CHAPTER 6 .... - 49 -
   COMMENTARY: 'MEETING MUSTS' .... - 54 -
   CHAPTER 7 .... - 58 -
   CHAPTER 8 .... - 61 -
   CHAPTER 9 .... - 70 -
PART 3 .... - 82 -
   CHAPTER 10 .... - 83 -
   CHAPTER 11 .... - 94 -
   COMMENTARY: PILLAR NO. 1 OF 'THE THREE PILLARS OF PERFORMANCE': .... - 100 -
   CHAPTER 12 .... - 103 -
   CHAPTER 13 .... - 112 -
   CHAPTER 14 .... - 120 -

COMMENTARY: 'THE 3 PILLARS OF PERFORMANCE: ACCOUNTABILITY' .... - 130 -

CHAPTER 15 .... - 134 -

COMMENTARY: 'THE 3 PILLARS OF PERFORMANCE: RESPONSIBILITY' .... - 139 -

PART 4 .... - 141 -

CHAPTER 16 .... - 142 -

CHAPTER 17 .... - 151 -

CHAPTER 18 .... - 158 -

CHAPTER 19 .... - 161 -

CHAPTER 20 .... - 168 -

COMMENTARY: 'CORE VALUES' .... - 177 -

CHAPTER 21 .... - 180 -

PART 5 .... - 189 -

CHAPTER 22 .... - 190 -

COMMENTARY: 'THE A-PLAYER GRID' .... - 199 -

CHAPTER 23 .... - 203 -

COMMENTARY: 'THE MEANING OF THE JOHNNY & JIMMY FABLE' .... - 211 -

CHAPTER 24 .... - 214 -

CHAPTER 25 .... - 216 -

PART 6 .... - 220 -

PART 7 .... - 223 -

CHAPTER 26 .... - 224 -

CHAPTER 27 .... - 229 -

CHAPTER 29 .... - 250 -

COMMENTARY: 'INSPIRE BY LOVE OR RULE BY FEAR' ..... - 261 -

CHAPTER 30 .... - 263 -

INDEX .... - 296 -

ABOUT THE AUTHOR .... - 304 -

PROLOGUE

On Tuesday, the surveyors moved in like bugs over the turf and scattered between the gentle curves of the land. Using state of the art equipment, they started the painstaking task of collecting three-dimensional data to use later in their graphical representations of the surface. Overhead, two gulls venturing too far inland cried into the wind as it swept through the scrub and the men's yellow jackets.

From a short distance, Lynne watched unseen, leaning back against the driver's door. The chilly gust reached her, lifting her hair and exposing the back of her neck to the cold; she dug her hands further into her pockets, bracing her shoulders against the bite.

It was hard to imagine this desolate scape of the North East playing host to so many visitors, athletes, delegates and businesses. Any company that could be a part of the excitement wanted to be, and for Lynne, her company's role was crucial. Losing out to another supplier was out of the question.

In her mind's eye, Lynne tried to construct the stadium and all of its spectacle that would lavish tourism and investment on the area, snatching the spotlight from the South for once and turning heads. She saw everyone in the crowd turning in unison as they tracked the athletes … and then she was there, hearing everyone gasp and erupt as she picked herself up from the landing mat, her arms raised in victory.

She shook her head free of the vision. She remembered so well how it felt – the joy of achievement and the solidarity – family – of the rest of the team. Still, not everyone can follow dreams. The competition was different, now, as her father would say. Losing was not an option. She must focus on what was ahead.

Erimus – "we shall be." The Latin motto coined for Middlesbrough in 1830 as the town committed itself to taking root and earning a respected area on the Great British map.

We shall be, Lynne swore under her breath.

And it was only Tuesday. She still had most of a week to get through.

PART 1

"The beginning is the most important part of the work."

PLATO, philosopher, circa 300B.C.

INTRODUCTION

The manufacturing company was the realised dream of Anthony Peston back in the late nineteenth century. It had been the bedrock of the family ever since, with each firstborn son taking over the reins in the traditional style every time, with one exception. In the late fifties, the firstborn proved to be 'incapable of leading', according to his father, and so the company missed him out completely and went to his younger brother instead.

There was no room in the Peston DNA for failures; whatever happened to that lad, nobody remembered nor cared. With several of the company's CEOs' being ex-military men, the Northern no-nonsense character traits of the business leaders took on a 'command and control' ethos that made them the toughest businessmen in the region.

Erimus Manufacturing was founded in 1878 just south of Middlesbrough, or "Ironopolis" as it was nicknamed, when the earliest blast furnaces were creating opportunities and new wealth all over the North East. The ironworks supplied the relentless demand for iron for the whole of the country's growing rail network, and in its heyday, the company had branches over the whole of Yorkshire.

Since the North had suffered the economic catastrophes of the 1970s, however, the number of branches had dwindled to just three. In Michael Peston's time, from 1987 until 2013, the company had clawed back some of its earlier success despite the slow economic recovery of the North East. With foresight, sheer grit and an ego that rejected failure outright, he'd made some canny investments and branched the business into new areas to keep abreast of changing, national demands.

It came down to hard work and a commitment to success. He had a belief in the virtues of the daily grind that was as hard as the steel his company worked with, and he made sure that his eldest daughter had it, too.

Lynne had been brought up in a privileged yet tough home. Neither she nor her younger sister were under any misconception that everything they had had come from the sweat of their father's brow, and that of his father, his father before him and before that. Privileges were earned, and they were both expected to be able to stand up for themselves and fight their corner with everybody on the outside. Their father was always the boss - at home, at his work and in the community. The family was well-known in the area; something of an institution with its inarguable history.

It's true that the Pestons had created work opportunities for many poorer families over the generations; several descendants of those families still revered them as demigods. As social circles and economic factors changed, though, the Peston name lost some of its lustre, with many people regarding their wealth and status with envy rather than respect, and several former business colleagues speaking openly about unethical business practices, corrupt lawsuits and even mythical criminality.

Still, other peoples' 'sour grapes', as Michael brushed it off, was merely a natural burden of success. Those jerks should shape up or ship out.

The flagship branch of the company was still based in Middlesbrough. Michael Peston had officially retired as CEO in 2013, while he retained his position as one of four directors. In practice, as his daughter Lynne had discovered, 'retire' was not a part of his vocabulary. In the months leading up to her taking over the reins as Group Managing Director, he'd threatened daily to just disappear to an island somewhere and leave this ruddy lot to drive the company into the ground. It wouldn't happen on his watch.

He'd had a lavish retirement dinner (on company funds, of course) and made a showy exit for the invited reporters from the regional press, and then reappeared at the office the next day for business as usual.

It had taken Lynne six months to finally move into her office. If she thought that it would be a simple case of moving him out and her in, though, she was badly mistaken. Michael still behaved as though he ruled the Erimus Empire, and was never short of a barked command or three.

She tried to ignore him, but it unsettled her. He made her stomach hurt.

CHAPTER 1

The boardroom door remained shut all morning. At five past one, it suddenly creaked wide and four grim-faced suits ambled out. They navigated the staircase and split into different directions in the open-plan office on the pretence of having something important to do. Their downturned mouths, hunched shoulders and vacant eyes told a different story, though.

Andrew was reminded of a line of shuffling vultures, choosing which bit of the carcass to go for first. Frankly, ridiculous. What was the point? It was always the same: a few hours in discussion, a few hours in reflection, another few hours in analysis and then a few decent people's livelihoods in the balance.

He kept his head down, made sure he sent out the signal that he was minding his own business. He didn't have anything to worry about, necessarily; they needed somebody to head up the manufacturing side of the business, and for the risks involved – especially with this lot – and his experience, why would they get rid of him? Still, you just never knew. He'd not been long in his role as Head of Department; just five months in. Enough to figure out who was who in the zoo, exactly what he had to do and, come to that, who did who.

Who gave a toss, frankly? He was far beyond the influence of office politics. Still, he could entertain the futile excitement of everyone who surrounded him; he remembered what it felt like – being a part of something exciting, unifying, edifying ... but teamwork is just an illusion. It's what you make of it. Eventually, you are what it makes of you.

Mincemeat.

On the other side of the desk divide, Roxy glanced up and met his eyes briefly. She flashed a quick grin at him and shrugged. The tension in the room was palpable, but it was just another day. She hardly ever knew what was really going on – the undercurrents and subtexts thankfully seemed to go over her head. The most she ever heard of the office gossip were whispered titters in the kitchen – half finished sentences from the corners of mouths, furtive glances and knowing looks.

She tried to ignore it all. It just made her feel nervous. Lately, she'd been struggling to get to sleep at night for the knot of anxiety in the pit of her stomach; every morning, bracing herself as she left her train for the short walk to the office, she wondered if today was the day when someone would find out how inept she really was. She had no problem dealing with clients and seemed liked by the rest of the team, but keeping up with the everyday incomings and outgoings in her care was a nightmare. She felt insecure – never sure that she was doing the right thing. Instructions and intentions were never really clear and the pressure was just getting worse.

Fortunately, the sales meetings were infrequent; they were supposed to happen every week, but so far she'd only been to three since she joined the company two months ago.

This morning, the mood in the office was even more tense than usual as the directors were visiting the branch. Apart from the brief acknowledgement from Andrew, nobody was interacting at all. Everybody concentrated on looking busy, calling their clients, working on their figures – and they were probably all looking more convincing to the circling directors than she did.

She watched Michael drift across the office, looking above everybody's heads, eyes focused on some spot in the middle-distance. Apart from his bulky frame, the family resemblance with Lynne wasn't easily visible at first. He seemed a lot more brooding – a big presence who didn't seem to need to say much to get his point across. She could imagine that he'd be quite terrifying to cross. Roxy wondered what he'd been like when Lynne was a little girl ... and then nearly giggled, as the idea of her boss as 'little' was hard to grasp.

Lynne speculated carefully through the large window of her office as her father shoved his hands in his pockets, meandered to the water-cooler and paused. He turned to stare vacantly at the floor for a few seconds, jingled the loose change in his pockets and frowned.

What was he thinking? There was no way she could tell what had happened in that meeting, but one thing was plain: today was a hell of a lot more significant than simply the usual 'quarterly catch-up'.

She turned back to her computer screen. Best to look busy. She could feel everybody on the floor watching her every move, trying to read her, see her thoughts. It's funny how you can always tell when somebody's watching you, even when they're facing the other way. She stayed still and concentrated on looking as relaxed as possible, pretending to type, while the whole left side of her body cringed from the staff's attention.

Bugger this. She'd brick up that window as soon as possible. This was like living in a goldfish bowl.

Suddenly her door was open, her father in her midst. She jumped, flushed in anger and embarrassment as one or two heads on the outside turned and watched, open-mouthed. Imagine just walking into her office like that without knocking!

"Fix me a coffee, that's my girl." Michael pulled out his e-cigarette from his inside jacket pocket and moved to look at the street outside.

"Dad, I'm just …" but it was too late.

At least three members of staff had overheard and were suddenly engrossed in their work, avoiding her and playing dumb as she found herself walking stiffly from her own office towards the kitchen. For God's sake – he was the one who had made her Group Managing Director. Why must he undermine her every time he 'popped in'?

It was no good speaking to her mother about it. That's where all this bowing and scraping rubbish had started in the first place. She'd never worked a day in her life – well, not paid, anyway – so how could she understand, let alone take her daughter's side? She had no idea why Lynne felt as though she had to wear different 'hats': one for family, another for 'Daddy's Girl' and yet another for 'Boss' of his beloved flagship branch.

Lynne waited for the microwave to ping and removed the about-to-boil half cup of full-cream milk, added the coffee grains and two and a half spoons of sugar before whipping it all together furiously into a froth. She topped it all up with boiling water, swearing as it splashed her hand.

There. Just as he liked it.

She threaded her way back from the kitchen, kicking Roxy's handbag out of the way and snapping at her to clean this joint up.

He was sitting at her desk, sucking on his ridiculous mega-vaper, billowing clouds of damp gas around himself like some kind of mock halo. It was a surprise that he didn't have his feet up.

She handed him his cup and awkwardly sat in the chair normally reserved for staff on the wrong side of her desk.

He slurped at it noisily and looked at her without thanks. "Those idiots don't know what they're talking about."

"What's been going on in there?"

"Confidential. No official decision, yet. There are still two points on the agenda for this afternoon and then we're taking a vote."

Lynne waited, started to count.

"Between you and me …" he tilted his head, dropped his voice and affected a conspiratorial tone. This time, it must be juicy. She'd only reached four. "It might be for the best. Show 'em what we can do when we're under pressure. Never liked that git in any case."

"Is this about Nicholas?" He was one of the four directors – a little weasel of a man who'd been with the company for longer than Lynne had been alive. Ostensibly one of father's oldest buddies, he'd fallen foul of Michael's tongue often enough over the years, mostly when he disagreed with him over some issue or other. Ever since she was a child her father had expostulated about him, usually at dinner. It made her nervous and she'd take more food. If her mouth was kept busy that way it couldn't get her into trouble. Recently, he'd announced that he wanted to retire and that the other three should buy him out.

Her father winced. "That tax issue last year knocked us harder than we thought it would. The company's not on track for recovery the way it bloody should be. You haven't achieved the plan – not any of you."

Lynne shrank in her chair.

"I can't imagine what you've been playing at, for God's sake," he kept his voice low, but the menace was there, itching to leap out of his throat.

The previous year had revealed a huge discrepancy in the company's results, leaving them with a massive tax bill that was forecast to take at least a year to recoup. With Lynne's branch being the main profit source, the onus fell on her to make up the difference, although all five branches were required to contribute. Staff members were laid off and cuts made in every department on every conceivable level. Although the problem had started long before she was made Group Managing Director, she was the one in the spotlight. It hadn't exactly improved her popularity.

"He's not leaving while we are making a loss. He wants what he calls his 'proper share'," he sneered. "We've got to get him out, of course, and he's giving us ten weeks to make the money to pay him off."

"How are we going to do that?" Lynne wished she could bite the words back as soon as she heard herself say them.

He glowered at her, now fully in boss-mode. "Well, now – you tell me. I put you here; you're the boss. You've got to pull this wreck together, get rid of the dead wood and turn it round. It's not for me to come up with all the bleeding answers for you all the damn time."

"Dad, I don't mean that. I just mean, it's a big deal to do all of that in ten weeks. That's all. Of course, I know what to do."

Michael leaned back and the chair squeaked painfully, straining with the weight.

"Are you sure about that?" he hissed. "I'm thinking you don't know your arse from your elbow, girl. I'm thinking I'm going to have to get you someone to answer to from outside."

Lynne paled. What did he mean, from outside?

"Someone who'll make damned sure I won't regret my decision to put you in charge. And when you've done it, you can pay me back in full for his services. You personally, not my company. Otherwise, this branch is done. We sell up."

Done. She felt sick. Sell up. Everybody gone - lost. Some bloke on her patch – another of her father's so-called old friends, ordering her about ... It was almost as bad as having her father himself back in this office. What the hell did this mean?

She gulped for air in shock, her mind reeling. It was pointless to argue.

He strode towards the door, spitting: "It's my way or no way. Ten weeks. That's all you get this time."

He left the door gaping wide behind him.

CHAPTER 2

Ian walked into the front room. Meeting the quiet head on was more disturbing than he'd bargained for. Every corner, curtain and colour was vaguely familiar, and thick with the chilly atmosphere.

Fleur-de-lis, paisley, swirls, twirls in creams, ancient forest greens, dusky pinks and God knows what – all claiming a bit part in history. It all surrounded him as he stood on the carpet – as far as possible into the middle to escape the tapestry of colour and power.

Many would call this ostentatious. Ian decided that he'd try not to call it anything. Michael was one of his oldest friends – well, an acquaintance, to be more accurate. This was not Ian's debut - he'd been here before. When they were boys at prep school, he and his classmates had come here a few times on special occasions – times for the locals to gather and celebrate with the most self-important family around. It had never been fun: too many rules and a strange sense of something just not being right.

He breathed in deeply and stood tall, his feet slightly apart, ready for whatever or whoever was about to enter stage left or right.

The time dragged by. A few minutes, at least. As his eyes grew more accustomed to the gloom, he picked out more details. The heavy Sanderson curtain draping the bay window. The oak panelled walls and heavy prints which spoke of years of family functions and dysfunctions. The empty stone fireplace that emanated stale woodsmoke.

The pale light drifting in from the bay window in the winter mid-afternoon light picked out the colours in the carpet and drew his eyes to the landscaped garden outside. A crescent of tiered stonework provided an elaborate rockery, and the remaining sticks and stumps of last season's plants cascaded down each level in a flowerless fall of greys, browns and khaki.

From his dimly lit vantage point, Ian surveyed the room. Without the lamps turned on or even the glow of firelight in the hearth, however, the corners of the room remained in darkness – shadowy crannies filled with whispers of past private conversations and muffled dramas contained within these walls from long ago.

He squinted into the corners, picking out a bookcase full of leather bound tomes in one, a small ladies' writing bureau in another.

Suddenly, the door to the garden swung open and his host burst in, coughing and wafting cigarette smoke away from his face.

Dear God!

How long had he been out there? Maybe the bastard had been spying on him for ages. Irritation crawled up from Ian's belly to the back of his throat, and he struggled to collect himself.

"Ian. My old friend." He stood quietly with his hands folded in front of him, like an unveiled statue.

The sudden splash of sound into the stillness of the room came as a shock. He straightened and braced himself for a difficult evening.

Thank God he hadn't opted for jeans tonight. Michael was in tweed, like some old time country squire, with his hair Brylcreemed back like Biggles. Ian had never seen anyone dressed like that on purpose and had to bite his lip as he hovered, facing him in amazement.

"Michael! Good to see you. How long has it been?"

Michael shrugged and waved the platitude away. He walked towards him with a glass of brandy in hand and clapped Ian brutally on the shoulder. Ian met his eyes and waited.

"I'm glad you came," Michael grunted. "Need you to take on a project for me. You've built yourself quite a reputation around here for improving companies' performances."

Not just around here, pal, Ian thought. His host was not in tiptop condition. His jowls hung down and gave the impression that his neck was exactly the same width as his head. His eyes were puffy and his complexion reddened through too many nights on that brandy, no doubt.

"What's on your mind?"

"Lynne's buggering it up. Took me years of hard work to build that company up and she's running it into the bloody ground."

Lynne was his eldest daughter – a recent business graduate who'd been given the title of Managing Director for Erimus Manufacturing when Michael had announced his retirement. It was a long-established company that had dominated the area during more affluent times in Middlesbrough. Ian suspected that Michael had given her the title and not much else. He was well-known for being bombastic, domineering and not a little bit disingenuous. Poor kid must be having a hard time of it.

"Tell me more about it and of course I'll look into it, see if I can take it on."

"'If?' There's a criterion?"

"Well ... I -" Ian stopped as a yell came from the dining room down the hall.

"That's dinner," said Michael, unnecessarily. Ian didn't argue.

He tried at least once to joke with Michael as they walked into the dining room together, but Michael didn't laugh. Ian read his host's tension; what could make a fully-grown man with a fearsome reputation in business and the community nervous in his own home?

The introductions in the dining room never actually happened. Michael, on edge and moody, glowered at his wife and daughters while Ian sat facing strangers. Ian took the lead and introduced himself to the assembled female members of the Peston family. He'd never been worried about finding conversation with anyone. The trick was usually to get them talking about themselves, and this bunch seemed to be able to do that easily.

He was placed opposite Michael's daughters Lynne and Fay, who shot him such a scathing glare of hostility as he sat down that he felt a very much like an outsider. Michael took up the carving knife and busied himself with it at the far end of the table, and so Ian was left to listen to the exchange between Brenda and her younger daughter. They were as self-focused as Michael was, blithely creating an uncomfortable environment for their dinner guest.

"But Mum, the Chanel dress isn't the right colour for my skin tone, and the Armani is too like Lynne's. I just don't like either of them, and that's that."

"Oh, for God's sake," Lynne muttered and pushed a spoonful of soup whole into her mouth.

"I see," said Brenda mildly. "Well, there's nothing else for it but a trip into London next week."

"Exactly. Give me your credit card."

Ian could offer nothing to the subject of ballgowns. He sat and fought the feeling of being distinctly unwelcome which had developed rather rapidly and was showing no sign of dissipating any time soon.

As the starters were cleared away, Michael rose from his chair and picked up the wine. The move opened up an opportunity for Ian to meet his hostess's eye at the head of the table, and he smiled.

She didn't.

He stopped and flailed about for something to say. He glanced at Lynne as Michael finished pouring her wine and moved around the table attending everyone else. Everybody's except Ian's, as it turned out. He simply missed him out, returned to his chair and filled his own.

"So, Lynne – how are you finding your role as Group Managing Director? You took it up last year, I hear?" Ian asked as he reached across and poured himself a glass of the wine. He didn't wouldn't let Michael play any of his passive aggressive mind games with him.

Lynne noticed what had just happened with interest as she reached for the salt and shook it liberally over a new spoonful of roast potatoes. She didn't have the same fascination for clothes and make up as her sister. Neither sister was particularly bad looking, but Lynne made nothing of herself and had the attitude of someone who was determined to show up her sister's attempts at grooming by packing on her own weight.

"Work's work. It'll be a lot better when I've got a better team. They're a bunch of lazy shites." She dropped her knife on her plate with a loud clatter and took a large slug of wine.

"If we have any more of this godforsaken weather I'll have to bring the bulbs in," Brenda aimed at the table in general. "They're miserable out there."

Ian imagined the mother was used to delivering a well-timed diversion or two with this family and continued to watch Michael with curiosity. He really must be nervous, Ian thought; he'd never seen him flustered like this before. This family of his clearly had an ability to push his buttons. He could understand why and almost felt a trace of pity for him.

Fay noticed and failed to hide a smirk. Ian resisted the urge to wipe it off her face for her.

"So – Ian, is it?" Brenda summoned him suddenly from the head of the table.

Michael looked up and grunted. Ian put on his sunniest smile as Michael answered for him. "He's here to discuss the Erimus management team. Bit of training – you know. Whip 'em into shape."

The whole table was silenced. Brenda gave her guest a hard look and spoke evenly. "How interesting. Well, it will be a godsend to get to the bottom of what's going wrong and get rid of the dead wood. From what I hear they are all a bunch of time wasters. Do you do a lot of firing for top businesses? Streamlining, don't they call it?"

"Oh, no," Ian laughed at the thought. "I'm more in the business of helping individuals and teams to find their passion, get on the same page and pull in the same direction. Then they can deliver great results. Of course, sometimes we might find we have the wrong people in the wrong seats, but usually it's the leadership that has to change its ways."

The room froze for about a year. Clearly, he'd said the wrong thing. He watched in amazement as Brenda turned away and started talking to the person to her right. Michael turned away, too and joined their conversation. Ian contemplated the roast beef on his plate and understood some of the challenges that would lie before him and the Erimus team.

The taxi dropped Ian off at home two long hours later. He sat in the living room for a long time nursing a single malt whiskey and a sunken feeling in the pit of his stomach. Wondering if he had bitten of more than they would let him chew.

For a family that is supposedly respected around here, they were pretty damned rude. Ian could understand how the attitude of the Pestons would make it very difficult for any of their employees to show their true worth. That thought fuelled his desire to work his magic with the team. If one evening's meal had been this unpleasant, he could only imagine what effect working for the family business would have on the spirit of those that did.

CHAPTER 3

Andrew liked getting into the office early. He'd never cared for open plan areas, preferring his own company and quiet concentration to the inane banter of others. How they expected him to think with all that din going on around him was beyond him.

This way, he could get the bulk of his difficult work out of the way before the menagerie arrived to scupper his morning. Figures and the boring stuff he could do with his eyes closed, but it was something he could pretend to be working hard at while he had to be in the office under Lynne's scrutiny. Come the afternoon, he could escape to the workshop, get a bit of peace.

On this Thursday morning, he was not the first in. Sean had beaten him to it, and he found him diligently tapping away at his keyboard at 7:40 am. He liked Sean. He was one of the quieter ones; Head of Marketing and a thinker, like himself. Over the last few months, Andrew had seen some of the ideas that Sean had come up with – packages that were sent out with the sales team, boosting revenue significantly. His creative mind was always thinking around corners – making the most boring of products positively exciting.

Andrew's staff loved the attention Sean gave them: manufacturing big plant machinery had never been thought of as sexy before. They enjoyed his visits to the workshop, ribbing him about this and that to show their appreciation of his thought and respect. Sean had put a spring in their step since he'd started with Erimus Manufacturing, and Andrew was glad of that. Hell, it was more than Andrew was doing at the moment. More than he could even be bothered to do, come to that. All the gossip and back biting had started to drain Andrew of his innate energy and flair.

He tapped Sean on the shoulder in greeting as he walked towards his corner desk. Sean glanced up and grinned.

"Now then," he muttered, tapping away.

In companionable silence, the two worked until the rest of the staff started drifting in at around 8.30. Roxy made a beeline for her desk opposite Andrew's. It was her worst day of the week. They were supposed to have a management meeting at ten but like so many things they weren't exactly regular or guaranteed. No doubt, Lynne would be in full force again, cracking the whip and making them all feel like crap. Roxy's stomach was always in a complete knot in those meetings.

The truth was, she'd never quite mastered how to report her figures - and she was Head of Sales and Hire. It seemed that whenever they managed to meet, Lynne would want the figures reported in a different way; what they had invoiced, what they had sold, what they expected to invoice. It was confusing and she relied heavily on the admin assistant that she shared with Andrew to give her the numbers the night before each meeting. Last night, she'd been up past midnight again going over them and trying to think of all the holes that Lynne might find in her report. As usual, she needed Andrew's support.

"Hey, mate," he greeted her affably, seeing her discomfort and feeling for her.

"Here we go again," she winced at him. "Wish me luck. If she shouts at me again I think I'll die. Coffee?"

He handed her his used mug, nodding his thanks with what he hoped was an encouraging smile. He wasn't holding out much hope for her. Many people had learned to use the confusion of the meetings to create a fog that Lynne couldn't see through but Roxy was too honest and straightforward to have worked that out so far. He put his headphones on and blocked out the office until the boss arrived.

Lynne navigated the top of the stairs and muttered something incomprehensible to nobody in particular as she burst into the office.

Andrew flicked his eyes up to the clock above his corner desk. 9:50 am. The meeting was supposed to start in ten minutes' time. She'd fiddle about with emails, news sites and a bite of breakfast before she'd eventually shift her fat ass into the boardroom for that, if indeed she did.

"Good night last night, lass?" Pete's impertinence made Andrew wince.

"Yeah, yeah – sod off and all."

Laddish laughs all round as Lynne backward-flicked her office door shut with her heel. Roxy rose to her feet as if impelled by magic and made her way to the kitchen again. As always, there'd be frothy coffee with two sugars, just the way Lynne liked it, with a second one on its way somewhere between now and quarter past. It was going to be a late start again.

Andrew sighed and shut down his email inbox. He may as well go for a fag.

CHAPTER 4

Andrew caught up with Sean in the rear car park. He called out to him just as he was rounding the corner to the back alley, his backpack bulging with his own pc equipment that he'd used since he joined the company, headphones and leads sticking out of the top in a messy tangle.

He turned around slowly, careful not to spill the contents of the small cardboard box he carried in front of him.

"Wait up. Where are you headed?"

"The station." Sean looked dazed and pale.

"Let's go to 'Mimmie's' first; I'll treat you to a coffee." Andrew lifted the box from Sean's arms and turned him around with his hand on his shoulder; they walked together. So what if anybody saw him from the window? This wasn't right, and he had to get to the bottom of what had just happened.

There were only three other customers in the corner coffee shop – none of them near enough to overhear. Andrew ordered two cappuccinos and joined Sean at the furthest table for two from the door. Sean nodded at him gratefully and cupped the mug tightly between his shaking hands.

"Have you ever heard of a 'protected conversation'?" Andrew shook his head. "She said it was a 'protected conversation'." Sean put his mug down and straightened up a little, gazing into it.

The shop doorbell rang and he flinched, reminded that Andrew was waiting for him to speak. He raised his face and looked at him, wide-eyed.

"Sorry, mate – I'm not sure what's just happened myself. Other than I've lost my job, that is." His poor attempt at raising even an ironic smile missed the mark.

Andrew waited, shocked. He could already feel his anger rising, but he had to hear what had happened to Sean first. This was just the very latest of a long string of unforeseen dismissals in the last four months: he had to know Sean's side of the story before he disappeared forever and the rest of the team was left to surmise the events. Tittle-tattle was destructive and pervasive. Andrew wanted the facts. He wanted this diligent young man to leave today less broken than he'd found him in the car park a few minutes ago.

Sean looked down at the table in front of him and thought back, straining his mind to focus on just one train of thought, blocking out all the questions, fears and images that were swirling about.

The morning had started ordinarily enough. He'd updated his log book of briefs in, briefs completed, each one's current status of production and taken it and his diary with him to Lynne's office for a 'catch up'. She hadn't been available for even ten minutes for an update in nearly three weeks now, and he was looking forward to showing her what he'd been doing and how he knew it had contributed to the execution of his strategy and the company's fortunes.

"Come in!" She answered his knock, and he entered her office, closing the door behind him.

"Morning, Sean – sit down," she nodded to the chair on his side of her desk and he put his ledger and diary down and sat, smiling in greeting. He was an easy person to get along with, phlegmatic with a 'can-do' attitude, and he usually managed to put people at their ease. Lynne didn't smile, however.

"I've brought you a copy of the workflow in Marketing over the past three weeks," he started, leaning in to offer her the information and talk it through.

"Actually, Sean, we're not going to have our usual meeting this morning. I have some news for you," she stated, matter-of-factly.

Sean was taken off-guard. He pulled his work back onto his lap and sat back.

"Let me start by saying that this is a 'protected conversation'," she flicked back her hair and straightened some papers in her in-tray. "The company's going through some very positive changes, making good progress into areas we've needed to explore for a long time and things are going well. It means that our structure needs to move with the times and we need to embrace a positive, new strategy of moving ahead of our competition." She sounded as though she were giving a press conference and reading a tightly-structured, meaningless script.

What was she driving at? Sean began to feel uneasy.

"You don't fit into that plan, so I'm letting you go."

He felt the blood drain from his face as the room rocked. He couldn't find his voice.

"In fact, you may as well leave this morning once you've finished here. There is no need to hang around. I suggest you leave straight away," she added.

Sean blinked. "Can I ask why?" He hated the way that sounded. It came out in a half-whisper, made him feel like an idiot.

"You're just not a fit for the direction we are going as a company from now on." Lynne paused, looking at him with an expression of ... of what? What was that look on her face? Sean couldn't make up his mind, but as time seemed to have slowed down to a crawl he had plenty of space to work it out as she continued:

"You look as though you're in shock."

Sean simply watched her with his mouth open. "Am I being fired?" he tried, clearing his throat.

"No, no – that would be putting it too harshly," Lynne looked uncomfortable. She looked away from his gaze and reached out her left hand to rest it on top of several folders that lay in her in-tray. It struck Sean as an odd thing to do, but then everything about this was odd.

"Then – am I being made redundant?"

Lynne raised her eyebrows. "No, you're not."

Surely it had to be one or the other? This didn't make any sense. Sean thought of what Helen would say; she still hadn't spoken to him since their argument two nights ago. She'd been right all along: there really hadn't been any point to his bringing all of that work home and working past midnight to deal with the overload. Now he didn't have a job at all. What would he do?

"I can give you my office for a few minutes if you like before you pack your stuff up and leave. We don't need you any longer and so we are letting you go; with immediate effect. You've been with us for less than twenty-four months, remember."

Then he understood. It was a done deal. He was expendable. She didn't feel he was worth of a fuller explanation. He wasn't the first and certainly wouldn't be the last. She was in battle-mode – and she always won.

Sean shivered as he remembered, and picked up his hot mug gratefully.

"What about your appraisals? Has anything come up lately that you needed to pay attention to?"

"Appraisals?" Sean laughed. "I haven't had one since I've been here."

Andrew groaned, but he wasn't entirely surprised. He'd had no appraisals himself, and still no answer to his three emails requesting the procedure for appraising his own staff.

" I wouldn't care but I've been working until two o'clock in the morning every night for the last week just to catch up on the backlog of work that we have going on. It seems that they were just waiting for me to catch up, like they knew I would. Talk about a 'pound of flesh'."

He stopped himself, shook his head. He slapped his mug down on the table and ran his fingers through his blond mop.

"Agh – what's the use. I tell you, mate," he said, glancing up at Andrew with a rueful grimace, "watch your bloody back, yeah?"

He stood up, grasped Andrew's hand briefly, swung his back pack into place and lifted his cardboard box from under his chair.

"Be seeing you."

Andrew watched him leave the coffee shop, hesitate for just a moment on the pavement outside before striding, head down, in the direction of the station.

PART 2

"Coming together is a beginning. Keeping together is progress. Working together is success."

HENRY FORD, business leader

CHAPTER 5

Ian arrived at the Erimus Manufacturing offices forty-five minutes before the scheduled meeting. He walked through the cracked glass door and started to climb the stairs, noticing the dull interior with no reception to speak of, no colour on the walls and not even a pot plant in sight. The stairs twisted away to the right and brought him to a solid-looking door with a bell, inviting him to 'Press for Attention'. So far, his experience had been less than warming.

After about a minute, a young man of about twenty-five opened the door, pale and creased. He regarded Ian vacantly, waiting for an introduction rather than offering one.

"Good morning – Ian Kinnery to see Lynne Peston. She's expecting me."

The young man held the door wide and Ian stepped into the most chaotic office he'd ever encountered.

Every desk in the open plan part of the office was covered in not just papers but tools, gadgets, bits of machinery, mascots and used crockery. The aisles between the desks were blocked by packets of printer paper, cardboard boxes, even a suitcase next to one particularly messy desk, as if the owner were planning an escape. On the windowsill at the far end of the office, a withered fern strained weakly towards the outside light.

Ian glanced around the faces in the room as he followed his escort towards a wall of windowed offices on the right. How did they face coming in here every morning? One or two looked up from their computer screens with tense expressions – not exactly unfriendly, but far from welcoming. He smiled and nodded at them, and then thanked the young man for showing him to the right place.

The door was the only part of the office walls that wasn't transparent. He could see Lynne inside at her desk – well, everybody could after all, and he wondered how she felt about that. Of course, she must have seen him approach, but she continued typing furiously at her computer until he knocked on the door.

She looked up, smiled briskly and moved to open the door.

"Hello, Ian," she projected, making some of the faces behind him look up and take notice. "Come in."

Ian followed, removing his jacket and a pile of papers from the chair on the near side of her desk before he sat down. With the offer of tea, the usual pleasantries and initial settling into conversation out of the way, he went straight to the point.

"Lynne, let's have a few minutes now to talk about the meeting at twelve," he said, evading any hint of an alternative.

She turned away from him and busied herself with rifling through her out tray, disposing of the paper in a tattered cardboard box that sat under her desk. She wasn't looking forward to the meeting; this coach had been brought in at her father's behest and she didn't like the way it made her look to her staff.

"I have a phone call that I have to make - can it wait until afterwards?"

Ian bit back his irritation and reminded himself why he was there. This was just a taste of the sort of thing she dished up to her team every day, so he'd have to take it slowly and firmly– not expect any miracles straight away.

"I think it's best that we talk now. Besides," he couldn't help adding, "I might be able to give you a way to save some extra, precious time for you every week for the next couple of months."

She laughed, challenging him straight in the eye.

"Go on."

"Here's what I suggest: while everybody is getting used to the idea of the regular meetings, I want to work on getting them used to regular involvement. A 'rhythm', if you will. The meeting is going to be their place to grow, and to start to work together, take accountability for their decisions and above all to learn to trust each other."

Lynne plonked herself down in her chair with something of a resigned air, although secretly she was listening intently for something she desperately wanted to hear. What it was exactly, she wasn't sure, but this conversation was a long way off 'conventional'.

"'Trust' each other?" She pulled a face. "How's that going to improve the figures, exactly?"

"You'll see." In fact, it was the key to their succeeding at all, but he was in no doubt that Lynne wouldn't understand – yet.

"They need to start to work together and to feel able to communicate with each other openly and honestly without feeling that they're ... well, on the spot. It's the first step in getting them to really care about what they're doing, and to invest more of themselves in their daily work lives."

Lynne was quiet for a moment, unable to hide the flicker of interest in her eyes. "So ... what does that entail, exactly?"

Ian grinned. "You're banned."

CHAPTER 6

At 12:00 pm, Ian was sitting in the boardroom on his own. He wasn't surprised; from what he could glean, nobody at Erimus Manufacturing had ever treated meeting start times with much respect. It was often one of the first noticeable symptoms of an dysfunctional team to an experienced coach, and he watched for it keenly at the start of every new commission. Although the answer to the problem was as clear as the table in front of him, it was often one of the most troublesome to correct.

It wasn't just that it was a bad habit that threatened productivity: it meant that the team had no respect for each other's commitments and priorities. It also undermined any possible cohesion of the team, as well as preventing the 'rhythm' of the office's weekly routine and, indeed, the meeting itself from being established. Without the necessary discipline, any synergy that could and should spring from the team working together would be lost, and life in the company would always be random, unpredictable and uncomfortable. His first note in the first five minutes of the first meeting with Lynne's team, therefore, was:

"Email – establish regular meetings and prompt attendance. Tuesday @ 12".

With nothing else to do, he gazed at his watch. The lopsided, plastic clock on the wall behind him told its own story. It had stopped at 8:25 – morning or night, who knew – and would remain unhelpful and neglected until somebody decided to change its battery, maybe even give it a clean. Ian wondered how long the clock had been like that and how long it would take for anyone to care enough to do something about it. He considered removing the old battery and putting it on the window sill to see if it would recharge a little – an old trick he'd learned when he was a kid. But the sun wasn't shining today, and beside it would be a good measure of the team's ownership of their environment. The flickering strip light over the far side of the table accentuated the dull walls, showing its plaster in places; in one patch, someone had patted two shades of khaki paint as colour tests before apparently losing interest.

How long ago was that? What had happened to the staff member who'd shown a glimmer of interest? He sighed, noticing the energy leaving him as he exhaled.

At 12:03, Roxy saved him with two cups of coffee and a big smile, handed him one of them and awkwardly chose a seat three down from his towards the end of the table. He thanked her, and politely asked how her morning had been. She was usually good at small talk, but she fell quiet with the sense of a new formality in the room, with its chairs arranged squarely in place and neat pads of paper each with a pen, and awaited her team members.

She was relieved when Andrew arrived with Natalie in tow. They, too, were silent as they took their seats, trying to look relaxed but both feeling out of place. Andrew studiously picked up his pen to headline and date the pad of paper in front of him. He glanced around the table and saw that the other two had brought their diaries, too. There hadn't been any email sent out to say what to prepare for this meeting; he hoped it wouldn't turn out to be just another rant on Lynne's part.

Fay drifted in at 12:06 pm, mumbled something that might be interpreted as a vague apology and sat down, looking bored, next to Natalie.

"Is that everybody?" asked Ian, rising to his feet.

Everybody looked at each other in confusion. There was an obvious absence.

Roxy giggled nervously. "Well, everyone apart from Lynne," she blushed, surprised at the sound of her own voice.

Ian moved to the door to shut it. "Lynne won't be joining us for these sessions," he announced, ignoring their astonished faces. "This is your time together. Even I'm not going to be around for many of them."

Andrew's jaw hung slack for a moment as he absorbed this. No Lynne? What the hell was this about? You couldn't have a management meeting without the Managing Director. Could you? It didn't seem right. This had better not be one of those trumped up, bullshit, New Age-type training programmes he'd had to get through before. Such a waste of time. They made his skin crawl. There'd be nothing worse than having to do bloody team games with this lot. He eyed Ian warily, preparing to hear the worst.

Fay burst out laughing. "Big Sis isn't going to like that much. Bet that wasn't her idea," she smirked, rocking on the back legs of her chair.

Ian smiled benignly. She was as much of a handful as her sister, that one. "As a matter of fact, she's completely on board with it. And," he couldn't help adding, "you'll soon get the hang of it. Surely you don't need her for everything."

Andrew snorted across the table; Fay looked like she'd kill him.

"So - welcome to our weekly management meetings. Every week we'll meet on Tuesday at twelve, so accept the invitation you've been sent to your calendars and make sure that you make a mental note of the time, too. This is your time, and it's to benefit you and each other, so prioritise it."

Everybody jotted the day and the time down. We'll see, Ian thought. In his experience, sticking to the start time wasn't among most unaligned teams' strong points.

"And please," he added, to give them a chance, "be here on time. The meeting starts at twelve sharp. Now – could you tell me briefly who you are and what your role is?"

As each of them introduced themselves, Ian wrote down their names and job titles. There was Andrew, Head of Manufacturing; Natalie, Head of Service and Repairs; Roxy, Head of Sales and Hire; and Fay, Branch Manager.

He sensed that the atmosphere was charged, perhaps with a little nervous energy mixed with curiosity, and he spent the next half hour asking them about their expectations for the effects that the meetings would have on each of their departments.

The job of this introduction was purely to set up the agenda for the following meetings, allow them to get used to the way he communicated with them and the way their own voices sounded in a meeting forum. From what he could make out, they weren't much used to contributing; he could imagine the sort of meetings they'd had with Lynne as leader.

The tension had dissipated by 12:45 p.m. with everybody explaining how things ran generally to Ian, and he in turn describing opaquely his role in developing management teams. He didn't want anybody jumping to conclusions about what he did, or how he was preparing to work with them.

"A colleague of mine will be joining us next week – Paul, who's an accountant and is doing some work with your financial team," Ian announced just before the team stood to leave. "Make sure you bring your figures for the month."

Roxy winced. She knew what that meant. Still, it was unavoidable, really. She shot Andrew a quick look and he gave her a supportive smile, and nodded to Ian as he left the room.

All in all, this meeting hadn't been as dire as Andrew had at first feared. It had eaten into his lunch break, mind you. At the thought of his sandwiches, he jumped down the last two stairs and trotted to his desk.

COMMENTARY: 'MEETING MUSTS'

No business can run successfully without successful meetings.

If businesses are about a team of people working effectively and efficiently together, then meetings must be an integral part of that process. Yet, for most of us, our meetings are boring, ineffective and to be avoided at all costs.

How do we run meetings that are gripping, effective and efficient?

I have learned over years of experience that there are three golden rules that, if we stick to them, will make our meetings at least effective and efficient. They are:

PURPOSE

AGENDA

TIME

I am referring specifically to a 'regular meeting rhythm', but these rules also apply in the most part to any other ad hoc meetings we might organise.

PURPOSE

I would never propose a meeting for a meeting's sake, but often this is how meetings develop. To counter this, I recommend that if you cannot define the purpose of the meeting in detail that you don't hold the meeting.

What is it that you are trying to achieve?

Once again, clarity is power. If you are very clear about the purpose of the meeting, you can be equally clear about who should attend, what the agenda should be and when it should be held.

"Begin with the end in mind", as Stephen Covey recommended ("The Seven Habits of Highly Effective People", Free Press, 1989). What do you want the outcomes of the meeting to be, specifically? What do you want to happen as a result of it? Why are you holding it in the first place? You cannot be too clear on this.

Think in ink. Write each idea down, so that any discussion can be measured against these pre-determined criteria to assess whether it should be part of the meeting or not.

When you are clear about the purpose of the meeting, you will be able to make better decisions about who should attend and pay attention to the second golden rule:

AGENDA

If you know why you are holding a meeting, you should be able to construct the 'agenda'. That way, people who are attending will know what they need to bring with them, how they need to prepare for it and what is expected of them at the meeting. This is particularly important for the regular, rhythmic meetings.

The agenda provides consistency and a structure. Meetings aren't meant to resemble a pressure cooker or a memory test. If you have gathered your firm's best brains together, you want them to be working at their optimum; make sure that you provide the environment which allows them to do so.

I recommend a fixed agenda for regular, rhythmic meetings, so that the attendees absolutely know what information they need to bring and they can be expected to be fully prepared for the meeting.

It should be constructed specifically to deliver the outcomes for the meeting that you have already decided. Type up your desired outcome at the top of the agenda so that everyone remains clear on it throughout the meeting.

You may think this is unnecessary, but answer this: how many meetings have you attended in which the purpose was not defined, and so forgotten or allowed to slip?

TIME

Not only do you need a confirmed start time, but you should also have a committed finish time, too. Otherwise, it's very difficult for your team members to manage their priorities. Will this meeting go on for one hour or three? Do them the courtesy of letting them know.

Keep the meetings as short as possible.

For regular, rhythmic meetings remember that there will be another one next week, the week after and the week after that.

I have noticed that when businesses begin having meetings, two things happen: firstly, there is usually pushback from the attendees. "Oh, not another meeting", they moan, and "We have so many meetings we can't get our work done". These objections are inevitable, but sticking to these three golden rules should minimise them.

Secondly, despite their objections, people tend to bring more issues to the meeting than there is time to discuss. Remember, you don't have to get through it all in the first meeting. You will have another opportunity next week and another the following week.

If you don't manage these two situations, the meeting will crash and burn and you will be further back than you were when you started.

Being able to manage meetings is a key skill for any business leader.

CHAPTER 7

From: Ian Kinnery
Subject: Tuesday @ 12

To: Andrew Willis; Roxanne Brooks; Peter White; Natalie Mitchell; Fay Peston
Cc: Lynne Peston

Good afternoon, All –

It was good to meet you on Monday and to see your offices. Thank you for your enthusiasm and agreement to take part in our time together. So that we can start the process in the way we should continue, we need to establish a few good habits from the outset.

To that end, please block off one hour every Tuesday at 12 for us to meet in the boardroom for your weekly management meeting.

There will be three items on the agenda each week.

1. Review of the previous week's and outstanding WWW (Who, What, When) commitments

2. Reporting of your departmental performance figures and compiling the company results
3. LB and NT

Don't worry that you don't know these terms just yet. You will do soon enough and they will make perfect sense.

To Your Success

Ian

Ian clicked 'Send' and waited to see that the email had been delivered. He stood up to stretch and stopped suddenly, arms out wide.

What the hell was that noise? He looked beyond the office doorway, past the kitchen and into the cluttered meeting room on the far side of the floor where Andrew was standing holding his mobile a little way from his ear.

Dear God – that was Lynne screeching at him. Ian could hear her from this far away. From the sounds of it she was giving him more than an earful, and Ian could hear much of it.

"Where the hell are you? Just who do you think you are? Stop behaving like a complete tosser and tell me where you're bloody going next time you feel like pissing off from the workshop! Who the hell are you with?"

Ian stood with his jaw hanging as he watched Andrew cowering and answering his banshee manager as though he were a chastised two-year old. What was she thinking of to berate him so loudly? Surely she knew that all of his colleagues could hear her? Why on earth was he having to take that kind of public abuse? If he wouldn't stand up for himself with this woman, how would he ever stand up for his staff?

If Ian was going to help this team to bring out the best in their people then he was going to have to keep Lynne out of the picture until she could learn to behave properly towards her leadership team. Otherwise, the leadership team would just exhibit the same behaviours their boss modelled.

Eventually, Andrew rang off and came sheepishly back into the office.

"Sorry about that. Same shit, different day." He rolled his eyes and tried a watery smile. He noted Ian's wide-eyed expression and laughed. "I can see you're a bit rattled by her already. She a nutter, but I can control her. Don't worry."

CHAPTER 8

At 11:45 am on Tuesday, Ian sat in the boardroom, pleased to notice that at least somebody had booked it for twelve with a piece of A4 paper sticky-taped askew to the outside of the door.

He tried to ignore the dreariness of the room and the rain dribbling down the window as he arranged the table. Regardless of the fatigue of the place, this was the room he'd been given to initiate change. He looked up at the clock, still insisting that it was 8:25 and shook his head. Just about any change around here would be a good one.

His wish was granted when, to his relief, all four managers arrived slightly ahead of time. This was a good start, and he was glad that he'd managed to impress upon them just how much their observing the start time mattered. Of course, they wouldn't understand the underlying effect of their observing the ritual for some weeks yet, but at least it was a positive start and they might be starting the 'forming' as a group. Beneath the flickering light, he could tell from their expressions that each of them had arrived with a reasonably open mind, and that was all he could ask for, for now.

Once the team had settled, Ian opened the meeting.

"Have you all brought your department's figures with you as I asked last time we met?"

Roxy's heart started pounding. Everyone murmured assent and started shuffling papers around.

"All I want to know for now is how much you have invoiced so far this month – that's turnover for now only. We're only at the end of week one so that should be a straightforward start. Then I can start recording how we're progressing over the next weeks. Andrew – would you like to start?"

Andrew leant back in his chair and waited for Ian to turn to a clean page on the flipchart behind him and write "Manufacturing" in the left margin.

"£5560," Andrew watched as the figure was written neatly next to the department name.

"Right. Roxy? How is Sales and Hire this week?"

"We're just about on £9000," she hoped she sounded more confident than she felt.

Ian turned to face the room and peered at her over his glasses.

"Is that the actual figure?" he asked. She flushed, and stammered a bit.

"Well, I'm aware of £8780," she stammered, "but I'm not sure if all of it has been invoiced yet."

Ian was puzzled. "Why not?" He hoped he didn't sound as though he was putting her on the spot; he was genuinely confused.

"Well, by Monday evening there was still an invoice to go out when I was given the figures. I don't know if it has been sent out today, yet."

Andrew started. "I didn't know we were including this week's figures," he peered over Roxy's shoulder to see her sheet. "I've just done mine up to close of play last Friday."

Ian replaced the cap on the marker pen.

"Same here!" called out Natalie. "I thought that's what we're always supposed to do. Aren't we?"

Fay patted her hair and leaned in to the table, wearing an innocent expression. "I always include stuff that I know has been signed off even if it hasn't been invoiced yet. I can't hang around waiting for another department to get its act together."

"So, Fay – what are you reporting this week for this branch, then?" Ian sat down again, picked up his pen and began writing notes on the pad in front of him. There was no point in writing these figures on the flipchart. Clearly, they were all out of alignment.

"£3970 as of this morning," Fay chirped, confidently. It was a good start to the month for the branch, all things considered.

There was a tense pause as Ian dutifully scribbled it all down. Eventually, he looked up and smiled at Natalie. He could sense that they all felt as though they were in trouble of some kind; well, all except Fay.

"At the end of Friday, we were on £2490 for Service and Repairs. That's this branch only," she added helpfully. "I only do this branch …" she trailed off as the painful pause returned.

Ian stopped writing, took off his glasses and regarded them all.

"Okay, so that's interesting. Why are your figures all being taken from different times of the week?"

They all looked at each other blankly. The light overhead flickered and snapped the silence.

"What is the process for your collecting and reporting your figures?"

"The 'process'?" Natalie frowned. "There's no special process, I guess. Some of us have an admin assistant who does it all for us – Andrew and Roxy, that is – and Fay and I do our own. As long as it's done before the managers' meeting every week, it doesn't really matter."

Ian could hardly believe his ears. Or his luck, come to that. Here was a clear place to start demonstrating what he was specifically here to teach them: that a non-judgmental forum in which they could discuss, share, debate and make some of their own decisions is the best place to form a balanced, happy team that's progressing, committed to positive change. It was very important that he didn't give them any of his own answers right now, and that he didn't come across as either domineering or patronising.

"Well, let's say, then – what was your situation by the end of last Friday, seeing as that's the earliest report we've had this morning."

There followed a lot of scratching of heads, paper shuffling and concentrated scribbling as each of them looked through the papers they'd brought with them. Ten minutes later, Ian was back at the flipchart, writing down the actual figures for each department as of last Friday.

"I'm happy to see those figures," he said, without commenting at all on whether he considered them bad or good. How would he know? "They're aligned. Readable."

"We can all see where we are on the page, that's for sure," said Andrew. He was beginning to feel a bit more switched on. This made sense, and it was a lot clearer than any figures reporting he'd been involved in at Erimus Manufacturing since he'd arrived at the company a year ago.

"So, can you each see your own and each other's situation clearly?"

Roxy smiled.

"Yes, even I can understand it so far."

The others laughed, remembering how she'd suffered the sharp end of Lynne's tongue frequently in meetings.

Ian remained composed, but inwardly was jumping up and down with excitement. The team was already beginning to talk – properly talk and share, not just respond to each other like robots, each in his own little world. Even Roxy had dropped her guard there, for a second. He took a breath and posed his last question for the morning:

"In that case, what do you think the process should be?"

Andrew leapt in. "We should close off the books at the same time for each department every week – probably Friday. And anything that isn't actually invoiced doesn't count."

There were nods all around the table as everyone scribbled it down.

"That feels good," muttered Fay to herself, although everyone overheard.

From: Ian Kinnery

To: Andrew Willis; Roxanne Brooks; Peter White; Natalie Mitchell; Fay Peston

Cc: Lynne Peston

Subject: Tuesday @ 12

Good morning, Everyone –

Thank you for attending our "Tuesday @ 12" meeting yesterday.

To you remind you of the one thing that we covered in the most detail that I'd like you to practice and keep up to date this week until we meet again:

- WHO, WHAT, WHEN? These details will always provide the accurate answer to the question "What is the process?". You need to know this for every task for which your department is responsible. This is the way to create the transparency the whole team needs to communicate and work together more effectively.

As an important reminder, please make sure that you take careful note of your INVOICED figures by the time you leave on Friday afternoon. Those are the figures you will need to report next Tuesday, as you yourselves have decided. Establish the habit now, and this will go a long way to clarifying what is actually happening figures wise in the company.

We had some interesting and helpful feedback on the "Liked Best" and "Next Time" sheets. Thank you for taking the time to do that. I'll share some of them with you next time, but in the meantime, please make sure that you put into practice whatever you mentioned as your "Next Time" goal so that you're ready for our meeting on Tuesday @ 12.

See you then. To your success,

Ian

MEETING: "LIKED BEST, NEXT TIME" (LB/NT)

DATE: 02/02

PARTICIPANTS: Ian K, Paul G, Andrew W, Fay P, Roxy B, Natalie M, Peter W.

LB	NT
Meeting started + finished on time	Bring 'aligned' figures for update - last friday close-off.
Cost saving from lessons learnt	
Successful contract review on target client	Agree "off-hire" process
1ST rigging container hired!	Start 'week end' reporting earlier
WE ARE A TEAM!! ☺	

THE "LB/NT" FORM

MEETING: "WHO, WHAT, WHEN"

DATE: 02/02

MEETING SUBJECT: Managers' Meeting

PARTICIPANTS: Ian K, Paul G, Andrew W, Fay P, Roxy B, Natalie M, Peter W.

WHO	WHAT	WHEN
Andrew	Instigate van inspection procedure for lifting gear.	Next week
Fay	Sort Sat Navs + seat covers for company vehicles.	Next week
Peter	Review month end procedure	Next week
Roxy	Look at options for holiday cover	Next week
Natalie	Find marketing company for outsourcing	2 weeks' time

THE "WHO, WHAT, WHEN" FORM

CHAPTER 9

Ian was first into the boardroom the following Tuesday. He liked to be early; it gave him a few minutes to visualise how he wanted the meeting to go. He smiled as he saw the sunlight streaming in through the mucky windows, allowing 'The Cave', as he had started to think of it, a direly-needed natural warmth and lift.

Within five minutes, his old friend and colleague, Paul, joined him, staggering a little with the awkwardness of carrying a large overhead projector through the doorway and past the chairs, neatly arranged as before.

"Thanks for coming," Ian smiled, immediately feeling a lift in his spirits. Paul was a good buddy – a solid type who could be trusted in situations like this, with a team that didn't already have all the answers and needed the encouragement and leeway to explore their own ideas.

For his part, Paul was used to Ian's methods, and understood completely that the most important thing that he needed to accomplish for the team to evolve was to remove fear. If the team felt that they were being judged by Ian, Paul or each other, there would be no openness, no transparency.

"No problem, mate. Where do you want this?" He set the contraption on the big table and looked around for a plug socket.

"I think we can use this wall, here." Ian moved to help him set up the projector, checking his watch as he did so. Nobody was late yet, but they were cutting it fine.

"I'm going to see if they're on their way," he said, leaving the room.

Paul laughed. He knew how Ian was a stickler for punctuality when it came to his meetings. If it were him, he probably wouldn't be too fussed if somebody arrived a minute or two late, as it always took that long for everybody to settle down in any case. But he and Ian were very different animals: he was a numbers guy, and didn't have the patience or the interest to get into all this human psychology stuff.

He had to admit, though, it worked. He and Ian had worked together on many projects and in every case he'd seen staff teams transformed by Ian's techniques. For Ian, somebody being late wasn't so much an irritation factor for him as a self-sabotaging habit which could derail the team's progress. Paul knew that, but still couldn't remember Ian's explanation as to why. He just liked watching him weave his magic until he handed over to Paul to explain the numbers. He switched on the projector and settled back to enjoy the show.

Ian found three of the group on the stairs. Roxy, Natalie and Fay greeted him as they passed and headed into the boardroom.

He reached the bottom of the stairs and looked around the open plan area. Andrew wasn't at his desk, and so he walked across the space and discovered him in the kitchen.

"Hi, Andrew – are you coming? It's two minutes to twelve. We're about to start the meeting." Ian stood in the doorway, interrupting Andrew as he was fiddling with the microwave.

He looked up in surprise, and turned to look at the clock.

"What about my lunch?"

Ian was taken off-guard, and it showed on his face. Surely, he'd made it clear how important it was that the meeting started on time?

"Well, I didn't think you meant, like, every week," Andrew started lamely, and made no effort to move from the microwave.

"Every week, Tuesday at twelve. Look, I have no objection to your bringing your lunch in with you if you'd like to, but the meeting starts at twelve – in one minute's time."

Andrew bristled, but knew deep down that he didn't have an option. For God's sake, he'd been working all morning and had missed breakfast. Since when were meetings so bloody regular and punctual around here, anyway? He stopped the microwave midway through heating his pasta, opened the door and put a plate over the top of it. He turned to Ian, shot him a dark look and walked past him out of the door.

That was close, Ian thought. It wasn't exactly a stand-off, but that little interchange could have ended decidedly worse. He took a breath and followed Andrew across the office area, watched him pick up his diary and pen and head for the stairs.

Still, it wasn't entirely unexpected. The team had warmed so far to the meeting rhythm— but Ian was aware that it might only be the "forming" at the beginning of the four stages of every group's development journey. That was normally followed by a "storming" of sorts – a moment when one or more of the team involved would resist the process, either consciously or subconsciously, and act in some way that could sabotage the flow of positive change. It was a natural part of the process, and any good coach, or manager, would always be aware of the undercurrents and tensions affecting the dynamics of the group.

Whether it was "forming", "storming", "norming" or "performing", any one of these stages would define the status of a group as it went through change. What's more, it wasn't a simple and linear process: as a group began to 'perform' well together, a new challenge could arise that would set them back to 'storming' again.

Indeed, all four stages would come at different times from different members of the team. Where more than two people are gathered together, there's always a degree of conflict: in itself, it's perfectly natural, necessary and not intrinsically bad. It was the coach's job to judge if it is 'good' or 'toxic' conflict and to keep his finger on the pulse of the group and be aware of these subtle changes as the group dynamics altered over time.

Well, he'd just witnessed an early episode of 'storming'. He knew it wouldn't be the last and he new that they would reach the 'norming' part soon enough.

Back upstairs in the boardroom, Paul was happily holding court with the three ladies.

"I see you've met," smiled Ian as he closed the door behind him and watched Andrew take his seat with a sulky face. "Paul, this is Andrew – Head of Manufacturing."

Paul reached over and shook his hand, settled back in his chair with a grin and prepared to watch the show.

"Paul is a friend and colleague who has agreed to join us for a few weeks to help us with systems and processes, particularly around the numbers. He is doing some work with Peter and the accounts team. He knows the way I work and he can save us all a lot of time in these early stages, I hope. Shall we get started?"

"Did you all bring your figures with you?" Ian asked, once the preliminaries were over. They all had, and Ian was pleased to see that they had all kept to the WWW of the previous Tuesday and were reporting on their respective departments' invoiced totals up to close of business on Friday.

Paul stood up and took a transparency, placing it on the lit window of his beloved projector. He still preferred using it to a laptop in meetings; he was a creature of habit and still did much of his work by hand whenever he could. He felt that the numbers looked more real and more dynamic that way than in print. Besides, the pens smelled nice.

Starting with Fay, he began recording the figures as each of the members of the team read theirs out. They were still only reporting on what had been invoiced. They went smoothly around the group with Paul adding each department's totals to the column. When everyone had had their turn, Paul was able to quickly add up the column and arrive at a total for the business for the month so far, up to Friday's close of business.

"So," said Ian, "What do the figures on the wall mean to you?"

"Well," said Roxy, "It is interesting to see them all together. It is the first time that I remember that we were able to see each other's numbers side by side. Normally by the time I have given mine I have forgotten everyone else's."

Everyone smiled.

"Seeing the company total is unusual too," Andrew added. "Before, we've never been shown the totals. I don't think Lynne liked us to know too much."

Fay jumped in. "You can see who is making the money and who isn't." Her area of responsibility appeared to have hit a purple patch; she wanted to make sure everyone knew.

"Now that you can see the company total what questions come to mind, I wonder?" Ian's question seemed to confuse everyone and the team fell silent once again. "Well, is the total that you can see good, bad or indifferent?"

"It looks all right to me." Andrew volunteered but the rest muttered that they didn't really know.

"What were the expectations for the first week of this month? How are we doing against our original plan. Against our budget?"

The sea of blank faces confirmed Ian's fears. They either didn't know their budget, or they didn't even have one.

"Budget?" Andrew confirmed his suspicions. "We don't have one. At least, not that I am aware of."

Ian turned to Paul. "Can you check with Pete and Lynne and find out where their budget is and why the team aren't aware of the company's expectations for this month?" Paul nodded, making notes.

Ian looked across the table. "Natalie, as you are keeping the WWW this week can you make a note of it please? Paul, are you OK for the 'when' to be this time next week?"

Paul was on familiar ground and replied "Sure. And if I can get something definite to you all before next Tuesday at 12 you will have it"

"Great. Shall we finish with the LB and NT as we did before? Can I have a volunteer to write it up on the flipchart?"

Natalie raised her hand, feeling like a kid in class. "I'll do it," she said. "Mine's the only handwriting that's clear enough."

Andrew laughed, and suggested that she might have a job for life as Ian turned over to a new sheet of pristine flipchart paper

"Let's start with the 'Liked Best' column – and I'll go first. What I liked best about today's meeting was that it started on time."

Andrew looked up quickly, but Ian ignored him and continued.

"What about you, Natalie?"

Natalie liked this sort of thing. "What I liked best was ..." she paused, trying to put her finger on how she felt. "I like the way we're all singing from the same hymn sheet now. Our figures seem more organised – it's good to see them clearly like this."

"Yes," Andrew agreed, "it feels like things are coming right. Even if they're not exactly where we'd like them to be right now, at least we can see them. The fog is lifting."

Ian laughed. It was a good phrase. Paul caught his eye and winked.

Natalie neatly wrote it down on the flipchart in front of her so that everyone could see.

Again, responses came thick and fast.

"It was good we can see the company totals."

"It was good Paul was here with his projector, so we could see and he could do the adding up!"

"It will be even better if he can tell us what numbers we are expected to achieve."

The banter was good natured and optimistic.

"What about the 'Next Time' column?" Ian prompted when Natalie had written all of the LBs down.

Andrew leaned forward and looked at Ian for a chance to speak. Ian nodded, pleased that he seemed to be on board again, his earlier chagrin set aside.

"I know what I wish we could improve for next time. It takes my admin assistant a whole day to get the figures together, and I have no idea why. Seeing as she does the figures for Roxy, too, though, that's going to be two whole days out of her week on just doing our figures."

Ian looked up at Paul. This is where his expertise might come in.

Paul cleared his throat and broke his silence. "Does anybody here know the system your accounts department is using?"

Everyone shook their heads. It had nothing to do with them; besides, it was probably way too complicated, in any case.

"This sounds like a 'Who, What, When' to me," said Ian, and all heads turned to him. "Andrew can you investigate why it takes so long for your admin assistant to get the figures for each of you?"

Andrew frowned in thought for a moment. "I suppose I could ask her and Peter in Accounts to meet with me and Fay. We could tell them why we need our numbers and find out if the system can be tweaked to do it more easily." He looked at Natalie who added it to the existing WWW.

"Good." Ian turned to the flipchart behind him. "By when can you do that?"

"I'll try for tomorrow morning. If it's doable, maybe things can be changed for this Friday's figures print-off."

Ian asked Natalie to confirm what she had written:

WHO: Andrew

WHAT: Arrange and have meeting with Admin and Accounts to discuss what needs to happen to get the weekly numbers more speedily.

WHEN: End of Weds morning.

"Good," he said. "it is on the WWW so we shall review it next week, and Andrew don't be shy to ask for Paul's input if you need it. This is his specialist subject after all"

Andrew looked a little shocked. This was a first. It was about time that the system started working for them instead of holding them up all the time. He wrote it down, and mentally started picturing himself having the meeting. Maybe he should book the boardroom for it ...

Ian thanked them all and let them go, glad that they were chatting animatedly together as they left. As their voices disappeared down the stairwell, he looked at his old friend grinning at him from behind his ancient projector.

"And the fog starts to lift," Paul said, clapping quietly.

COMMENTARY: 'THE FOUR STAGES OF GROUP DEVELOPMENT'

The 'Four Stages of Group Development' are fairly well known and documented. Sometimes referred to as 'Tuckman's Model', the four stages are 'forming', 'storming', 'norming' and 'performing'.

'Forming' is the initial phase, when the group first comes together. Everyone is excited and buoyant, looking forward to the task and the times ahead; it can be almost euphoric in its nature.

Inevitably, 'forming' gives way to 'storming', when reality bites and individual styles and preferences start to clash. The pervasive storming phase often catches the new or naïve leader by surprise. It is perfectly natural and totally inevitable, so it's important to just push on through this phase as it will eventually give way to the 'norming' stage.

The 'norming' stage is where the group starts to develop its own norms. The members decide for themselves how they are going to work together; their core values develop and they start to mature as individuals. They decide what sort of team they are going to be – say, a 'Manchester United' or a 'Hartlepool United'.

The 'norming' stage gives way to the 'performing' stage, where the group is now set to perform at its best.

All groups pass through these four developmental stages. It's worth pointing out that, although the progress is linear, it's not necessarily sequential. It may well be that the group, having 'formed' and 'stormed', then reverts to 'storming' ... and so the progression begins again.

It can be argued that any change at all in the team can set them back to phase one, or an earlier phase for them to start the journey anew. Arrival at the 'performing' stage is not the end of the journey, as they will inevitably be provoked back to an earlier developmental stage by some event or other.

PART 3

"A collection of talented individuals without personal discipline will ultimately and inevitably fail. Character triumphs over talent."

JAMES KERR, author

CHAPTER 10

The group filed up the stairs, chattering and laughing. Andrew was the first one to the top, and his hand stopped over the door handle to the boardroom.

"We'll have to find somewhere else," he said, turning back to his colleagues, now collected at the top of the stairs.

"What's the matter?" Ian shouldered past the others and drew alongside him, peering through the narrow window into the room.

Lynne sat at the boardroom table with her back to the door, her laptop open and a bowl of soup steaming next to it.

"Lynne's working in there ..." Andrew awkwardly stated the obvious, keeping his voice low.

Ian kept his expression neutral. "Did anybody book the boardroom for today?"

"I did," answered Roxy, half raising her hand as though she were back in school and quickly finding her hair to fiddle with instead. "I thought it might be a good idea to have a Boardroom

Diary downstairs so that everyone can see when it's booked. I guess she didn't get the mail …" she trailed off, worried that she'd just made her boss look bad.

"Then you'll have to ask her to leave the room, Andrew."

He had to be kidding. Andrew looked straight into Ian's eyes and saw no trace of irony there. He laughed nervously and shifted from one leg to another, glancing back through the door at Lynne's back.

"But we can use the office area just as well -" he began, and stopped.

"These are the rules. Every Tuesday at twelve, in the boardroom, for everybody here without fail. Not only do you all know that, but Lynne does, too. Now, ask her to leave the room."

Andrew took a deep breath and gingerly knocked on the door just before opening it. Lynne jumped at the noise and spun around.

"Yes?" She noticed the group behind Andrew and frowned a little.

Andrew peered at her, wide-eyed and reddening behind his glasses. He lent into the room tentatively and barely whispered, "We – er, have a meeting in here … booked the room …"

"Oh, right. Of course, yes – I'll just …" Lynne was on her feet, snapping shut her laptop and sweeping papers, her diary and the soup up in one go, splashing it a little as she untangled her feet from the chair.

Andrew watched in amazement, glued to his post at the door. She'd been as embarrassed as he. As she manoeuvred her bulk past him in the doorway, he sucked his stomach in and tried not to notice that her face was just five inches from his.

With his heartrate continuing to rise, he stumbled into the boardroom, elated and shocked at her apparent submission. What the hell had just happened? His face turned bright red and he faced Ian with an expression so startled that everyone laughed.

Ian grinned at him. "Right – let's get to it. Come in everyone, and sit down quickly."

With the attention of the group redirected to the matter at hand, Andrew sat down and hid his shaking hands under the table. He hadn't felt this supercharged in years.

Ian waited for them to settle. "Natalie, can you make a note for the Who, What, When please?"

She looked at him quizzically.

"The meeting started on time," Andrew smiled, adding, "against all odds!"

"Well done Andrew, the weekly management meeting is the most important event of the week, and everyone should know it," Ian was pleased.

As he scanned the room he noticed a new, fresh face at the table. This must be Pete, the accountant and part of the leadership team. He had been on holiday when the weekly meeting rhythm had begun. Ian had been grateful for that: of all the managers, Pete necessarily worked closest with Lynne. Establishing the meetings' rhythm and agenda would be easier without them both.

However, Pete was back from holiday now and needed to take his rightful place at the meeting. He needed to be fully aware that things were different now. He welcomed Pete, saying that they had established a new, professional meeting rhythm and that he needed to be aware of what it was all about.

Turning to Roxy, Ian asked her to start bringing Pete up to speed.

"Oh, well," she began nervously, "we meet every Tuesday at twelve for our 'Tuesday at 12' meeting," the others laughed, encouraging her. "We all have to be here ready to start by twelve. There are three items on the agenda: 'Who, What, When', the numbers and 'LB and NT'. We all have to have our stuff ready."

"It sounds like code" replied Pete. "What is a 'Who, What, When' when it's at home?"

"You'll soon get the hang of it," assured Andrew. "It's how we record our decisions for action. We follow it up the following week and we expect the person accountable to have done what he, or she, committed to."

"All very formal," Pete commented.

"Well," said Andrew, "that's what we all commit to, and if you want to be part of this team it's what we expect you to commit to, too, or we'll kick you off the team." The broad grin showed that Andrew was threatening Pete largely in fun, but the heaviness of the words and the nods from his colleagues more than hinted that the comments weren't made purely in jest.

Pete noted a new seriousness about his colleagues and decided he wouldn't be the one to let the side down.

The meeting followed its now established pattern and so they moved through the agenda ahead of time. Rather than let them go early, Ian resolved to do a little impromptu coaching with them all.

He asked for permission first and followed with, "What do you understand by the word 'autonomy'?"

"Power!" Pete answered immediately, with a glint in his eye.

Ian opened his mouth to congratulate the newcomer on his contribution, but was cut off.

"More like freedom to do what you like," interjected Andrew, "although maybe that's just splitting hairs."

Ian shrugged and encouraged them. They were in a great mood today. "Neither is quite right … although it's true that freedom and power do come into it. Anyone else?"

"Governance." Everyone turned to look at Fay, who held her innocent expression until Pete grabbed her mobile phone from her hands.

"Yeah – she's just looked that up online," he teased, waving it around.

Ian was pleased that the mood in the room was relaxed, convivial. It made forward progress so much more likely. Creating synergy between the members of the group was made possible with the right level of energy in the room. This was a marked difference from the previous meeting.

He smiled. "Well, independent governance, if you like ... but how would that relate to each of you at work?"

There was a brief silence as everyone took a step back from volunteering a suggestion.

Andrew found himself enjoying the discussion. His mind had felt so dog-eared lately that he was amazed at how little effort it took him to speak first.

"Would it mean each of us is responsible for our own activities? Like, we have to make decisions for ourselves?"

"As opposed to having them all made for you, yes – I'd say that that is exactly what it means. But it's less a case of your having to do it, and more a case of your getting to do it. What about 'mastery'?"

Pete frowned. This should be a meeting to discuss what was going on with the team, not an English lesson. What was Ian driving at?

"That's exactly the same, isn't it? Autonomy, mastery – same diffs."

"Well, no ..." Roxy seemed surprised at the sound of her own voice. "It's not really the same. Mastery is about a level of expertise, too, I think. becoming very good at something. You have master craftsmen don't you"

"Absolutely," Ian nodded and turned away from the group to write on the flipchart behind him. He took a green pen and wrote the words 'autonomy' and 'mastery' in large letters. "One more," he announced, and wrote 'purpose' boldly underneath. He replaced the pen and turned back to the group.

Andrew looked up from his notebook. "Aim. Motive!"

"Reason why," Roxy ventured, only to be interrupted by Fay.

"Doing something on purpose means doing something deliberately, rather than by accident."

"Good. Yes, all of those answers are important," stopped writing and turned back to them. "All three of these words are going to become the most powerful words in your vocabulary soon. Over the next couple of months, you're going to see yourselves develop autonomy, mastery and purpose both as individuals and as a cohesive group. We're going to use these times together to encourage growth in these areas specifically; once you focus on these three things, the rest of the show comes together."

He watched everybody write the words down religiously, and noted their concentrated expressions. Without knowing it, they were encouraging each other to learn; to absorb this new information.

This was promising. It meant that things were beginning to move forward. A team that learns together grows together.

If Ian could help them develop autonomy, mastery and purpose they could transform themselves from a haphazard bunch of people who happened to work in the same firm to a team of competent, committed leaders who knew how the business worked and cared how it performed.

Just imagine, he mused.

COMMENTARY: 'THE THREE DRIVERS OF TEAM HAPPINESS'

Happy teams are productive teams. That's a fact.

But that is not the only reason why you, as a business leader or a business owner, should pay attention to your team's happiness.

You should pay attention to your team's happiness because it is the right thing to do; because people matter and because you can. Individuals and teams are happiest when they feel like they have some control; when they feel as though they can make their own decisions.

The three drivers of team happiness are AUTONOMY, MASTERY and PURPOSE.

People and teams enjoy becoming more capable and competent in their roles. They like the feeling that they are getting better and reaching a place of mastery in their craft. They like to feel that they are part of something bigger – a part of something that matters, something more than just themselves.

To me, these three concepts are obvious. They are self-evident: they resonate with me and make real sense.

Personally, I despair and rail against decisions that are made for me and in which I have no say. I love to be a part of a team. I value growth towards mastery and one of my stock definitions of happiness is that "Happiness comes from progress. Progress shows up in the form of growth and a sense of contribution." Purpose is important: it's about being the best we can be for reasons that transcend the day-to-day, the here and now. If you've found your purpose, you're blessed.

Although the three concepts of autonomy, mastery and purpose are obvious, like so many things they are not commonplace. Whilst they're widely understood, they're not so widely practiced. So often, both leaders and their teams reject autonomy. Many leaders feel a need to make the decisions for the rest and so often the rest shy away from the opportunity to make their own decisions. The reasons for this are obvious and counterproductive.

Frequently, leaders fail to allow their people to develop the level of mastery that they should or could; equally, we see individuals spurning the opportunity to become true masters of their craft, preferring the more populist route of mediocrity. What's more, leaders are often unable or unwilling to address the higher purpose of the work at hand; individuals convince themselves that work is drudgery and has no evident, higher purpose.

These symptoms result in unhappy, disengaged, underproductive and ineffective teams. Surely, we can be a little more enlightened than that today. After all, with every pair of hands comes a free brain.

I have the privilege to work with and coach teams every day, and in the process, I can almost guarantee their growing sense of autonomy, mastery and purpose. It is little surprise, then, that I see their level of happiness rising with every encounter. It strikes me as being the ultimate win:win.

An old adage sometimes attributed to William Penn says, "I shall pass through this world but once. Any good, therefore, that I can do or any kindness I can show to any human being, let me do it now ... for I shall not pass this way again."

CHAPTER 11

Andrew made sure that he had a good breakfast that Tuesday morning before he drove into work. He wasn't prepared to get caught again as he had been last week, and it was a long morning without food. The last thing he wanted was his stomach to start growling like a bear in the middle of one of those long, awkward silences that always seemed to happen after Ian asked them a question.

Those questions were the worst bits of the meeting. Ian only ever seemed to ask really obvious, basic questions – 'what is the process for X?', or 'what day of the week do you have scheduled for Y?' - but for some reason nobody ever seemed to be able to answer them. It made him feel like he was in school, except this time with no clever kids putting up their hands in the front.

He laughed at that. If he felt like a dunce in these meetings sometimes, then so did the others. The idea of Fay's being taken down a peg or two made up for it, at least.

The thing was, though, Ian himself never pointed the finger at any of them. There was no accusation, sarcasm or making an example out of anyone. No threats, come to that, either. He was privately amazed that Lynne had picked him to take on their development; her own techniques, if you could call them that, were the polar opposite to his. How did she know him?

He liked the calmer, drama-free version of the management meetings. And he liked that they happened at the same time every week, especially. The 'Tuesday @ 12' meetings, as they had come to be known from the regular subject line of Ian's emails to the team, had become the focal point of the week for them all. Such a simple way of unifying them. It wasn't so much rocket science as repeat science; the fact that they actually did it every week now made all the difference to the team and seemingly the business.

He felt a little embarrassed about the incident last week at the microwave with Ian; that wouldn't happen again. Hence breakfast: another obvious solution to an avoidable problem.

He reached over to the stereo and turned up Neil Young as he sat in bumper to bumper traffic. This stretch was usually a bit snarled up, but he was in good time and a good mood this morning. He hadn't listened to this album for years.

At ten o'clock, Andrew picked up his hard hat, protective glasses and earplugs at the door of the workshop floor and tucked in his tie before walking into the area. He was expecting the usual cheery round of greetings and biscuit-offering, but this time was disappointed.

The energy in the large space was electrified. People who were standing around at the edges next to their equipment were still, eyes trained on the corner of the workshop floor where a cluster of their teammates fretted and fussed over something on the floor.

He went cold. Please don't tell me this is what it looks like, he prayed.

A couple of the workers looked up and pulled away as he approached, revealing a crumpled Charlie Foster half-reclined in an old oil patch on the floor, rocking backwards and forwards in agony and groaning – his face screwed up with the effort of holding back a tsunami of his most colourful language.

"Charlie? What's happened? Where are you hurt?" Andrew noticed with a thump in his chest that his worker's hard hat was missing. He glanced around and saw it lying upside down about three metres away.

Charlie couldn't answer. He was puce in the face and merely looked up at Andrew, nodding in the direction of his right foot, where two female staff were busy fiddling with his boot.

"Stop – don't interfere with it," commanded Andrew, and they stopped immediately, looking shocked and scared.

"He was working on this section, pulling the shelving backwards, and knocked the spare equipment that was stacked at the back next to the wall. It came down on his foot," Mark offered from somewhere near Charlie's head.

"We wanted to get his boot off – it must have taken a pounding. That winch weighs a ton!" Barbara gasped, clearly wanting another go at the boot.

"Has anyone called Emergency Services? No?" They were relieved that Andrew was taking control. "We're going to keep him comfortable until an ambulance arrives. Has anyone seen the incident file?"

Barbara scrambled to her feet, glad of something helpful to do. "It's in the office," she garbled, halfway across the floor already. "I'll grab it and make the call!"

Andrew knelt behind Charlie to let him lean back, try to relax. He looked at his watch and made a mental note of the time: this would have to be documented properly. He cursed under his breath as he looked around the area, especially into the corners and against the walls where spare parts and heavy machinery were stacked up, poles, metal bars and large tools loosely propped vertically with wires undone, stretching and knotting like spaghetti across the floor.

This had been an accident just waiting to happen. It was a nightmare version of the mess in the main office space upstairs – full of hazards. His arms and back started to ache with the strain of keeping Charlie balanced. He was looking extremely wan – now with his eyes closed, a sweat developing on his brow and his breathing coming irregularly and shallow, intermittently bracing and gasping.

He waited an age for Barbara to show, who nodded at him as she jog-trotted back to the scene of the accident, indicating that the ambulance was on its way.

Shit. He was in for it now.

By a quarter to eleven, news of the accident had reached the main offices. Lynne paced up and down behind her closed door, biting her thumb nail and worrying about insurance.

The thing was, as Andrew had pointed out, the equipment that had fallen and hurt Charlie was not supposed to have been there. It had been standing loosely, instead of its having been packed and stored away properly. That in itself could pose financial problems for the company, let alone there being a member of staff injured and presumably off work for God knows how long.

Shit. She was in for it now.

Roxy caught up with Andrew in the car park at the back of the building, where Charlie had been trussed up like a bird for the oven and popped neatly into the ambulance. The paramedics had been great – not just stabilising and pacifying Charlie himself, but instilling more of an air of calm on the workshop floor, too. Andrew was grateful for that, and turned to Roxy with a preoccupied expression in his eyes but less of an adrenaline rush, thankfully.

"Here you go," she said, handing him a cup of tea. "Poor Charlie – poor you! You've done what you can now, though. Try not to worry too much, mate. Let's wait and see what the hospital says."

Andrew had never had to deal with an accident on-site before. Damn it – why had he allowed that bloody workshop floor to be in such a mess? He'd inherited it that way five months earlier, it was true; but why had he had to wait for an accident to happen –

and possibly a bad one – to a valued staff member before it occurred to him to do anything about it?

Damn. Damn, damn, damn.

"Sure." He appreciated Roxy's support, but really wanted to be alone right now.

As the ambulance drove out of the parking lot, Charlie now informed that his 'missus' would be at the hospital to meet him, Andrew turned and strode towards the door, forgetting to hold it open for his colleague. She watched him take the stairs back to the office area two at a time and really felt for him. She could see Lynne in her mind's eye, lurking in wait as he entered the office, jaws at the ready.

Holy cow. He was in for it now.

COMMENTARY: PILLAR NO. 1 OF 'THE THREE PILLARS OF PERFORMANCE':

AWARENESS

We cannot fix, improve or develop something of which we are unaware.

If we are unaware that we do not lift our tennis racket high enough on the serve, or that our demeanour appears cold and hostile to some people, or that prioritising the urgent over the important is jeopardising our chances of achieving our goals, we are helpless to change them.

Sir John Whitmore wrote, "I am able to control only that which I am aware of. That which I am unaware of controls me. Awareness empowers me. No two human minds or bodies are the same. How can I tell you how to use yours? Only you can discover how, with awareness."

Profound words indeed. That which I am unaware of controls me! How much is there of which we are unaware? We may be unaware of certain facts, like the bigger an organisation gets the more complex it becomes, that growth sucks cash, that managing millennials is different to managing fifty-somethings. We may be unaware of behaviours such as our becoming domineering, scared or impotent when we are stressed; that we listen less and shout more when we are enthused; that our ability to read the signals from others is poor or badly calibrated. Being unaware limits us, controls us, renders us 'stuck'.

Conversely, awareness is curative. Once we become aware of something, human nature and inventiveness may kick in and we can often adapt and develop our behaviour quite naturally and independently in a more helpful and productive fashion.

Those moments we refer to as 'light bulb moments' or 'Aha!' moments happen when we have become suddenly and unexpectedly aware of something of which we were previously unaware. We are surprised and startled by the discovery. Right then, we often decide to behave differently in the future.

Sometimes, these epiphanies are all the more surprising because we feel that somewhere in our being we were aware already; deep down, we already knew. This is the difference between our being unconsciously aware and consciously aware. Unconscious awareness is fine, but conscious awareness allows us to think, reflect and choose.

Often, as a coach, it is my role to take something in the client's unconscious thought process and allow him the time and the space to hold it up to the light of conscious scrutiny and to make thoughtful choices based on a heightened awareness. After such conversations, I am often met with the words "it's just common sense!". It is, but common sense isn't that common – much less commonly practiced. When we know something, it is obvious. When we don't, it is an impenetrable mystery.

When I use the phrase, "we don't know what we don't know", I am often referring to the fact that we aren't aware of that which we aren't aware. How could we be? Tiger Woods said that he retained his coaches because he couldn't see his own swing. None of us can.

How many things are there in your life that you are unaware of and that being unaware of renders you helpless and stuck? Of course, you can't answer that question; imagine, though, how different you might find things if your awareness were to be increased suddenly and accurately? How much closer to your true potential could you soar? How much more easily and effortlessly could you navigate the seas of life and business?

Awareness, accountability and responsibility are the pillars of performance and it all starts with awareness.

CHAPTER 12

As Roxy disappeared through the door, gingerly reaching to pull it closed behind her while balancing her coffee mug, Ian swung into the parking lot. All of the places save one was taken, but that one was half occupied by Lynne's massive SUV which she'd parked at a careless angle.

He called out through his window.

"Roxy – will you ask Lynne to move her car? I can't park in the space she's left for me and I don't want to have our meeting interrupted by someone whose space I've had to park in."

Roxy nodded at him, looking worried. On top of everything else, now she had to face the storm upstairs. Life could be cruel at times. Still, none of this was her fault. She knew it, but couldn't help feeling tested and frightened of what was going to happen.

As she climbed the stairs like a martyr, it occurred to her that she spent a lot of her time feeling ridiculously guilty about things she hadn't done. Just this morning on her way in, she'd felt herself blushing and slowing down in the left hand lane as a police car overtook her. Why? Was there a stash of weed in the boot? No. Was she even breaking the speed limit? No. Was her registration plate skew? No. She just had that crushing sort of conscience that some people have – mostly her female friends, come to think of it – that made her feel inadequate in every possible situation. Her inner dialogue seemed to be the voice of a nasty, aggressive bully.

God, it would be nice if it would just shut the hell up sometimes.

She stole into the office area from the back staircase and dragged her feet towards the din that was emanating from Lynne's office. That voice sounded very like the one in her head.

Lynne was it the midst of tearing into Andrew for lunch. He was standing quietly, just watching her, apparently waiting out the attack.

Should she wait before knocking? If she did, Ian would merely sit in the car park until Lynne went out of her own accord, and Andrew might lose a limb.

Taking a deep breath, she knocked on the door with the energy of a moth.

Lynne saw her rather than heard her and scowled.

"What is it?" she snapped.

"Ian asks if you could move your car, please," she whispered. Come to think of it, he hadn't said 'please'.

"For Christ's sake!" Lynne fumed, grabbing her keys and barging past them both on her way out.

Andrew looked at Roxy. "Cheers," he said. "I was running out of oxygen holding my breath."

Ian walked into the office and turned immediately to mount the next flight of stairs to the boardroom floor. Of course, he'd noticed the icy atmosphere as soon as he entered the open plan area, but he held his expression and kept walking.

Paul was already in the boardroom, teasing his beloved projector's focus into submission and humming to himself.

"Morning!" Ian greeted him. "Any idea what the drama is about downstairs?"

Paul had no idea – and was pleased to be able to say so. Ian cast an eye around the table to check that everything was in place, and they waited for the team to arrive.

Fay arrived first, pulling a face and using a slapping action with her hand to show that there was trouble on its way. Ian smiled his hello and pretended not to notice.

She was followed by Roxy, Andrew, Peter and Natalie who arrived altogether. It was perfectly obvious who was at the centre of it all: Andrew was camouflaged in nearly the same shade of magnolia as the wall behind him. Ian welcomed them all as usual and kicked the meeting off with the all-important follow up of last week's WWW.

It had been Andrew's mission to arrange a meeting with Peter from Accounts (present, Ian was pleased to see) and his admin assistant, whose bad luck it had been until now to have to piece the figures together for each report. Had they managed to come up with a solution between them?

"I had the meeting with both of them on the Wednesday morning as we said," Andrew started, lacklustre. Natalie started scribbling the update down. "It seems that there was an issue with the software that Accounts was using that wouldn't allow for anyone outside of the department to access the files. Pete – can you tell Ian what you told us?"

Pete stood up to address the room. He'd been waiting for a chance to add his bit to these meetings.

"It's something that the Accounts Department put in place several years ago. At that time, the sales team could access the files, and a few of them were changing them to make their revenue reports look better."

Ian blinked. Paul stifled a laugh as he looked at his friend's face. He bet he knew what he was thinking.

"So, we arranged it with IT so that they couldn't access them anymore. From then on, they had to request whatever files they needed from us."

He went on to explain that on Wednesday morning he'd met with Andrew, Roxy who was Head of Sales, their shared admin assistant, the Head of IT and Paul to come up with a solution.

Andrew picked up the last bit of the follow up report. "Now, there's a way that Sales and the other departments can see and print off their figures, but as a 'read only' file. That way, nothing can be tampered with once Accounts has closed off each Friday."

Ian was pleased. He looked around the table and could see that everyone was happy with the result.

"Nice work," he said, paused for just a moment: "So why the long face?"

Andrew smiled ruefully and inhaled deeply. The poor man looked like he was going to be sick. Everyone automatically looked down at their papers, giving him personal space to say what he had to say.

"There was an accident on the shop floor this morning. Quite a nasty one. One of my team has been taken to hospital for surgery on his right foot."

Ian was sorry to hear it. He could understand that Andrew would be upset but was still a little confused as to why this had seemed to crush Andrew's spirits quite so badly. Accidents happened on workshop floors. Just how bad was it? Was this the first time?

"Well, for the company, no," said Andrew with delicacy, "but the thing is, it could be viewed as the company's fault. There was so much equipment lying around, and it was one of the smaller winch cranes that landed on him. It shouldn't have been there."

Ian felt for him. So that was why he looked like he'd just been savaged and hung out to dry. Figuratively, he had been by Lynne, no doubt.

Everybody started to talk at once, all agreeing on one point: the workshop area needed to be tidied and sorted more professionally and more safely, and so did the office space, come to that. There might be an accident just waiting to happen in there, too.

Ian was on high alert as things started to descend to a mudslinging match. Raising his voice over the sudden hubbub, he drove them straight to the point.

"So whose responsibility is it to see to the safety and tidiness of that particular area of the building?"

"It's Andrew's, naturally," Fay shrugged innocently from her end of the table.

"It's not like anyone's ever done anything about Health and Safety, here," said Natalie. "He inherited that workshop floor and the state it's in just a few months ago. And as far as the office area goes, who's ever bothered keeping that tidy? It's chaos in there. It's chaos everywhere. It can't be just one person's fault."

Roxy agreed. "Hear, hear. Besides, who here has ever actually completed that 'Health and Safety' course thing we were all supposed to do when we joined the company? Not me!"

They all looked around at each other and shook their heads.

Paul interrupted from the projector. "Don't you have to sign off a sheet to say that you've read through the health and safety part of the induction, though? It's not long – should take only a couple of hours; you can't muck about with stuff like that or you'll not be insured properly, you know. That's potentially really serious."

Ian waited for a response. Finally, it came from Natalie. Turning red, she said in a low voice, "I remember that I signed it without actually reading the stuff through. I had too much else to do."

"Me too," said Roxy.

Fay shrugged. "So who has the time for all that extra paperwork in any case?"

Again, Ian let the silence fall. They all knew what had to be done. Let them come up with it.

Eventually, Andrew spoke.

"If that's another "Who, What, When", it's got my name on it again," he said, not quite smiling, but a little less fatalistic than earlier. "I will take accountability for that whole area. Someone has to and it's my patch after all. But it will take me longer than a week."

He picked up his pen with sudden resolve and wrote in his own diary.

"Natalie, please record that I will have that job done entirely by this time next month. I will have all of my area clean, tidy and above all safe"

Ian noticed with pleasure that his face had turned to the right colour at last.

MEETING: "LIKED BEST, NEXT TIME" (LB/NT)

DATE: 04/05

PARTICIPANTS: Ian K, Andrew W, Fay P, Roxy B, Natalie M, Peter W.

LB	NT
Meeting started + finished on time	No Sat Nav for vehicles
More confidence in forecast figures	Reply "All" on emails
Improved visibility through systems	Procedure for stock-take
Forecast increase in last week	Not enough promo material – make up gap in the Marketing Dept.
AMAZING order win from targeted client !!!	
Shop floor passed inspection	
Acting on "Who, What, When"	

IAN KINNERY

MEETING: "WHO, WHAT, WHEN"

DATE: 04/05

MEETING SUBJECT: Managers' Meeting

PARTICIPANTS: Ian K, Andrew W, Fay P, Roxy B, Natalie M, Peter W.

WHO	WHAT	WHEN
Roxy	Arrange meeting with Lynne re mark ups + sales prices	Next week
Roxy	Advertise Sales role	Next week
Natalie	What is Dom's role in "Service Engineering"?	Next week
Andrew	Produce log of all test equip. + include valuation	Next week
Fay	Conversion rate for test-bed quotes	Next week

THE WWW FORM DIRECTS PROGRESS

CHAPTER 13

Should she or shouldn't she?

Roxy stared at her risotto steaming away on the stove. It was either this and another five hours' struggling on her own with a bottle of red over her figures for the next day's meeting, or the other.

The other would take the risotto and the whole bottle of wine to pluck up the courage to do, though.

She looked at the kitchen table, strewn with her files and pieces of paper covered with numerical scribbles. Whether she did this right now or had dinner first, it would still be there. Let's face it, the meeting was just over fifteen hours away. The moment when she'd meet her doom.

She'd better have at least a semblance of professionalism in place, or she'd be fired without a shred of dignity. That was not going to happen if she could help it.

Sighing, she flicked off the hob, pulled the pan off the heat and grabbed her coat. She swept up all the papers in a brusque grip, shoved them altogether into her laptop bag and headed for her front door.

It was going to have to be the other.

She decided not to warn him she was on her way over; she needed his help and this was the only way to get it – with the element of surprise.

Andrew sat on a pile of tatty scatter cushions he'd chucked across the floor, investigating an old suitcase full of LPs. Out of all the boxes he still had to unpack from his move nearly six months ago, this was the least important. He still didn't know where half of his bedding was.

But hell, it was by far the most fun.

Led Zeppelin, Pink Floyd, Steely Dan – they were all there just waiting for him like old friends. He picked up *Steely Dan*'s "*Countdown to Ecstasy*" and smoothed the cover with the flat of his hand.

Go on. Why not? It's time.

He was quite surprised at himself. This was the first time in years that he'd felt like listening to his music. He stood up and went to the cupboard under the stairs, searching for a big box with "Fragile! Handle with Care!" scrawled on the top in thick black pen. It was underneath two others at the very back, and by the time he'd uncovered his old turntable, amp and huge speakers, the place looked like it had on the day he moved in with boxes all over the living room floor.

There was a knock on the front door.

Andrew stood still for a second, puzzled. He looked at his watch: 9:25 pm. Who'd be pitching up unannounced at this time on a Monday night?

He unlatched the door, being careful not to open it too wide so that whoever it was couldn't witness the mayhem within.

Roxy stood on his doorstep, woolly hat in place, waving a bottle of something and carrying her laptop bag.

"Surprise!" she trilled, trying vainly to raise a smile from him.

Andrew was more stunned than surprised. He stood for a moment, taking it in. How did she even know where he lived? Ah, yes … she'd brought his company car to him on his first day at Erimus Manufacturing, and he'd driven them both back to the office.

She had a good memory.

"Hey," he started, unable to keep the edge of panic from his voice, "what brings you here?"

He opened the door wide for her, and she picked her way through the obstacle course of boxes that blocked them from the living room. She looked at him quizzically.

"Yeah – I know it looks like I've never unpacked. I had. Well, I hadn't, but …"

He was flustered about her catching him with his home in a mess, she realised. She quickly made him feel at ease.

"Oh, my God! You've got a turntable!"

Distracted, Andrew pointed to the albums in the old suitcase in excitement.

"You've arrived just in time for a music appreciation evening," he joked, rather pleased with himself.

She handed him the bottle with a grin and threw her laptop bag onto the shabby three-seater. "Don't worry," she giggled at his shocked face, "there are only papers in it. I'm afraid I'm here to ask for a bit of help, too."

He understood now. It was her figures again. He'd never known anyone get into such a tizzy about them before reporting. She probably wouldn't get any sleep tonight knowing that the meeting was coming up at twelve tomorrow without his looking them over with her.

Her department's figures were trickier than most. Roxy was Head of Sales and Hire; quite apart from there being two distinct strands of revenue for which she was accountable, the pressure that was placed on her personally by Lynne was greater than on anybody else. Roxy's department had to perform like puppets at times, and although Roxy had done much to stabilise things, the staff turnover historically had been sky high.

The way to prevent that, Roxy knew, was by hiring execs who had the right work ethic and the same core values as the company in the first place, and then by training them religiously, often, forever. But then again, who knew what the core values of the company were? It was a standing joke in the office that nobody there had seen them except Lynne, and she'd forgotten them.

"It's not so much that I don't understand it," Roxy explained. "It's just that I can't make out the language of the accounts reports themselves. What applies to what cost? And whose revenue are we talking about in this column? There are so many codes I don't know where I am."

"Yeah, I know what you mean," Andrew poured the wine, handing her a glass. "Sit down and relax, talk me through what you've got as I put together the sound system. It can't be that bad."

You little know, Roxy thought miserably.

She took off her shoes and pulled up her feet underneath her, grabbing a few of the scatter cushions from around Andrew's place on the floor and cosying herself into the arm of his sofa, taking a sip of wine and looking around.

He had more taste than she'd assumed. She didn't know a lot of blokes who went in for artwork, but he'd found himself a few retro prints of something or other ... not bad, and they added a splash of colour around the room. It's funny seeing a colleague's home for the first time, she thought. It's like discovering a whole new side to them.

Andrew was busy twisting the copper threads from the speaker wires to thread them into the back of his ancient amp. Nothing wrong with that little beauty, he smiled to himself. He began to feel the old excitement come over him – the same feeling he used to have every day when he was a youngster. What a time that had been: rock concerts, endless parties, friends around all the time – and, unlike his mates, a job he really enjoyed and that paid handsomely.

He should have known that all good things come to an end. It had been a bit of a crap lesson, that one.

Roxy was saying something about Lynne. He pulled his attention back to her and listened.

"I'd rather put up with Lynne than have to look elsewhere. I know she's a pain in the ass and I have to confess, I feel sick in the mornings when I wake up just knowing I have to face her each day. Do you ever feel like that?"

Andrew looked up at her, gave a slight nod. Things had started to improve for him, he'd noticed. Maybe it was easier for him pretend that Lynne was genuinely out of the picture when he didn't have to deal with her daily as Roxy did. Now that she wasn't joining them in the management meetings, either, he could avoid her completely if he timed his visits to the workshop floor cleverly enough.

"If you feel that godawful, Rox, maybe you really should start working on your own exit strategy, though. Allowing yourself to get that stressed out isn't good for you. Believe me – I know," he rolled his eyes as he remembered his previous job.

Roxy wanted to hear more, and paused for him to continue. He didn't.

"One place can be just as bad as the next, I guess," she went on. "But no, it's not that. I have a younger half-sister who's pretty much dependent on me right now. I truly cannot afford to lose this job – for either of our sakes. She's at college. We lost our parents a few years ago."

Andrew was quiet. How had that happened? It seemed like an awful lot of responsibility. Wasn't that like being a single mum?

"Lord, no," laughed Roxy. "First of all, she's twenty and capable of looking after her bloody self, and secondly, she doesn't live with me. She's in digs. She's dependent on me for rent and food, though. I made a deal with her that if she gets through all of her exams with flying colours first time round, I'd pay her keep until she's finished."

"What's she studying?" he asked, smiling at her happier mood.

"Accountancy," Roxy said, taking a sip of wine.

They looked at each other for a second, and then both burst out laughing.

It was only once they'd finished the bottle, polished off a large packet of crisps that Andrew had found somewhere in the depths of his kitchen cupboard and gone through all of the lyrics of *The Dark Side of The Moon* that the dismal subject of the next day's figures came up again.

Roxy was pulling on her coat, preparing to meet the taxi she'd called to collect her.

"Well, tomorrow should be a right laugh, anyway," she said, glad of the warmth the wine was giving her. "My department's already cocked up the forecast for the month. I'm four grand down."

Andrew winced. "Look, it's no good hassling about that now. You've done what you can, and you have to agree, Ian isn't a bit like Lynne."

"Yes, but he has to feed it all back to her, doesn't he? It's not like she doesn't know what's happening to her bottom line."

Andrew pulled the gravest face he could.

"If she really knew what was happening to her bottom line," he said seriously, "she'd shift it to the gym."

Roxy laughed loudly and gave him a spontaneous squeeze. He didn't resist, and patted her a little awkwardly on the back. He opened the door for her and saw her into the waiting cab, waving her off with a smile that lasted several minutes.

CHAPTER 14

The meeting on Tuesday at twelve rolled around too quickly for Roxy's liking. It seemed that only a couple of days had passed since the last time she'd found herself sitting in the boardroom with the others, shaking for at least ten minutes before it was her turn to report her figures for that week and the month.

All in all, she enjoyed the meetings. It felt good to listen to the others speak and share what was going on in their departments. It was even better to know that she wasn't the only one who faced several sticky situations every week, and she liked hearing how the others were really doing. Perhaps everyone had been wearing a bit of a front until now; in the meetings, there was a transparency that was entirely new and it made her feel less of a fraud.

However, forecasting was still a nightmare. She'd had to do it twice now, and she was no more confident that she was going to hit her self-imposed target than she was at the start. In fact, she was sure that she wouldn't. Today was the day when it was going to come out into the open.

There would be trouble, she was sure of that. It wouldn't be the first time she'd screwed up.

She edged into the boardroom and immediately noticed that someone had fixed the strip light bulb. Great – that's all she needed: more light shed on her shoddy performance. Its incessant flickering had always irritated her, but why had it been changed for today, of all days? She took her place next to Andrew – he was always good at making her feel more steady – and hid her financial papers underneath her A4 diary.

"Good morning, everyone," Ian smiled around the room as they all responded. "Thanks for being on time – Natalie, you can make the first entry on the LB/NT form 'meeting started on time" again!"

They all laughed, used to the regular meeting pattern now. After working through the WWW of the previous week , they turned to the figures. Peter took over the recording of them at the projector from Paul, and the image of them appeared clear and large on the wall next to the door in his neat handwriting. Meanwhile, Paul sat back from the table, taking notes and observing. Things were beginning to settle within the group – they were 'forming', and he could sense it. This might be the last meeting he'd need to attend, but, as ever, he was completely absorbed with what was going on around him as the 'observer'.

Ian was happy with the atmosphere in the room. He was beginning to feel as though the group was starting to 'pull' the agenda forward rather than his having to 'push' it onward. He focused on keeping his questions in tune with the natural turn of their conversation, prompting them to examine issues more closely only if it seemed that they were missing an important point. The most innocuous of questions had the power to create a significant learning opportunity, as they had all seen for themselves the previous week. Andrew in particular had noted it and had suddenly sprung to life.

The turning point – his 'Eureka' moment - seemed to have happened when he had volunteered to take ownership for the "Who, What, When" regarding the accident that had taken place on the workshop floor. Such a simple tool to deal with so many improvements and solutions to unforeseen problems! At last, they were deciding as a collective who was accountable for what and by when – moreover, they were all answerable to the leadership team, to themselves, not to anyone else. It seemed strange that there were fewer shouting matches, fewer rants and yet everyone felt more accountability to each other and to the business He felt energised and involved, and was becoming a surprisingly good influence on the rest of the team.

Right now, he was giving an update on his findings from the workshop floor.

"Like I said," Andrew chatted on, "it's going to take me a couple more weeks to get the floor sorted out properly, but everyone seems to be on board now that Charlie's been hurt and they're all taking some responsibility for keeping their own stations tidy and clean, and reporting anything that seems wrong directly to me. We're getting there."

The others gave him a spontaneous round of applause and he grinned. This was so much better than before. He was getting better sleep at night, too, and perhaps it wasn't entirely down to the fact that Lynne was keeping out of his face for a while. Long may that last.

No, there was something else: he genuinely looked forward to getting into work in the mornings, and these days drove in listening to his own music rather than listening to bad news talk radio.

"How is Charlie, anyway?" Ian asked, noticing the exchange of smiles between him and Roxy.

"He's getting better – he'll be on crutches for a while and so he's not allowed on the premises. He's been put on sick pay for four weeks, which hasn't pleased Lynne much."

Ian imagined her tearing a strip off Andrew for that. Sure, the responsibility ultimately came down to him, but Ian had a feeling that the one who was giving him the most of a ticking off was Andrew himself. He liked things to be done right; this accident had happened on his watch. Ian hoped Andrew had the sense to live in the moment, do what needed to be done, learn from the experience, forgive himself and move on.

"So, onto the figures," Ian suddenly announced, and he smiled directly at Roxy. She was looking like a rabbit caught in the headlights as usual; best to put her out of her misery. Lord, why did she hate this part of the meeting so much?

"Roxy, at the beginning of the month you said that your department would bring in thirty grand by the end of it. Last week you were on ..." he glanced down at his paperwork. "£12300. Firstly, what have you brought in this week?"

Roxy coughed and straightened up.

"Eight thousand three hundred," she said, looking up at him with wide eyes. Well, this was a good start. She'd sounded precise and confident with the figures and by all accounts had only nine thousand four hundred to find in two weeks to deliver her prediction. That should be easy. Things often picked up towards the end of the month.

"Okay, well done. So what is the forecast now? Ian expected it to have moved forward given the running rate.

Roxy could feel the tremor in her voice as she announced "Twenty-six thousand."

Ian glanced up at her over his glasses. She cringed.

"Twenty-six? that has moved backwards four thousand since last week."

Roxy wished she were anywhere else but here. The nightmare was coming true. She braced herself for the battering, took a deep breath and stared down at her hands.

"Well, yes," she started to explain. "I had included one invoice for the hire of equipment to one of our regular clients. It was invoiced at the start of the month. Credit Control started to chase payment for the invoice. The client said that they'd taken the equipment 'off hire' at the start of the month. They refused to pay the invoice, understandably, and so we had to raise a credit note to reverse it. That's why we have moved four thousand backwards

This process was entirely correct and appropriate, but Roxy looked thoroughly miserable.

"Well, first things first," Ian decided practicality was the way forward. "Where's the equipment now?"

"It's with the client still, but it's being collected this week."

"Okay, good. Well, that leaves your department with a shortfall from your original forecast. You still have two weeks left of the current month and your running rate is strong. You have achieved twenty thousand six hundred in two weeks. Do you think you can get back to the original forecast?

Roxy looked up, surprised. This was a new tack. Lynne would have said, "You have two weeks to find that four grand or you're out! Nobody's indispensable!" She thought for a moment and allowed a note of hope back into her voice.

"Well, there is something that I was going to forecast for next month that I might be able to bring forwards; the client's working on a project faster than expected," she scribbled the note down in her diary to chase it directly after the meeting.

"So why did you choose not to bring that in to your forecast today Roxy?" Ian asked with a calm, level and curious tone.

"I was worried. I knew that I had messed up with the last forecast I gave when I found out about the credit note and I didn't want to overpromise again" Roxy admitted.

Ian laughed gently, which took Roxy by surprise.

"Look, your forecast is part science and part art. You will know what orders you will have coming through to be invoiced. That is the science part. It is your job to get as much delivered and invoiced as possible. You should be constantly scanning your order bank and working with your team to get everything delivered. That is in your control"

"The part that is art, is estimating how much of your current activity is likely to result in invoiced business this month and next month. So, your forecast will never be one hundred percent accurate. It can't be, but the better you know and understand your business, the more accurate it is likely to be."

"It is important that you are as positive and optimistic as possible. Your forecast is really your commitment to the team and the business so having made it, we all expect each of us to drive very hard to achieve it or better it. But I would warn you against being foolishly optimistic. If you are forecasting results that have no chance of being met you will only be demonstrating that you don't know or understand your business and the results of your activities as well as you should. You will be deluding yourself and the team."

"In many ways, you are saying that this is what my part of the business is going to throw into the hat this month. Use it to get your department committed to it and go for it. Have fun with it. Don't stress about it. It wasn't anyone's fault that you didn't know about the credit note, but as we get better controls in the business I promise you there will be fewer surprises like that."

"Shocks, you mean," Andrew interjected, lightening the mood further.

Roxy stared at the paper in front of her, feeling strangely relieved and emotional; she bit hard into her bottom lip. Don't cry – don't you bloody well cry, she yelled at herself. Ian's words rang in her head as she concentrated with all her will to stay calm and professional, at least on the outside. Did he really mean all that? Could forecasting be a positive tool to benefit her and her team, rather than yet another impossible task that Lynne would use to verbally beat her up about?

When she was ready, she looked up at Ian, who continued without fuss, accusation or drama.

"it is just another set of skills that you will develop. In a week or so you will be wondering why you ever found it difficult"

He gave her a quick, respectful nod. It was Roxy's department to run, and she was perfectly capable of understanding her responsibility. For him to give her a telling off - as he was sure Lynne had done in the past -would have been humiliating for her, which would in turn have only served to make her angry and fearful. Ian knew very well that fear makes people react badly: the staff would either lie, or eventually leave. The outcomes would be equally as bad.

Roxy breathed, and was grateful for the conversation's moving on. As she sat quietly digesting this new idea, she felt her confidence creep back with every breath she took. The sense of fear and tension leaving her body was almost tangible, and she wondered if it were noticeable to anybody else in the room.

What the hell, she smiled to herself. I don't care if they see it. We're on the same side, anyhow … and suddenly she felt the tears gripping and twisting the corners of her eyes again. She shook herself, and concentrating on what Ian was saying.

"Before we move on, though," Ian caught their attention before Andrew prepared to report his figures, "there's something we need to address here. There's an obvious and dangerous hole in the system."

Fay, who'd been a bit surprised to hear about this, spoke up.

"Tell me about it! There's a client who's been sitting with our equipment for the best part of a whole month who's not even using it, let alone paying for it! We could have hired it out to another company by now. God knows how long that could have gone on!" She slapped her pen down on the table and leaned back, rolling her eyes.

Andrew glared at her. She could really be like her sister sometimes.

Ian moved quickly to defuse the situation. He ignored Fay's arrogance and desire to apportion blame and moved to address the issue of the fault in the system instead.

"What is the process for 'off-hiring'?"

There was a long silence.

Well, that speaks volumes, he thought. There probably wasn't a robust process – or perhaps any – in place.

He asked each manager in turn what their department would do in a similar situation and, of course, was given a different answer each time. That meant that one company had four different processes in place for the same operation.

Everyone was quiet at the realisation. Even Fay had the wind knocked out of her sails. This was an extremely uncomfortable revelation. Until now, nobody had bothered to find out what other department heads did, each choosing to look after his or her own situation in isolation. For the most part, it wasn't an attitude of selfishness, as far as Ian could make out. It was more a case of self-preservation: nobody cared or dared to stick his head over the parapet. Better and far safer to keep a low profile. Inevitably this lack of working together was to the detriment of the business and the systems.

It was a reality check. Once they'd considered it in silence, Ian refocused his disillusioned team.

"Well, okay. What does the company's Procedures Manual say? Do we have a way of dealing with this situation that's already been written down?"

Again, the silence was deafening.

"Sounds to me like that's a 'Who, What, When'. What's the 'what'?"

Natalie picked up her pen and pulled a 'Who, What, When' form towards her. "The 'what' has to be to check the Procedures Manual to see what the correct one is for 'off-hire'," she said confidently, scribbling it down.

"That's right," Ian nodded. "So ... who's going to take that one on?"

Then came the biggest surprise of the morning. Without a second's hesitation, Roxy raised her hand.

"I will. I'm the one with the most vested interest right now in any case."

Ian smiled and nodded in approval. Andrew gave her a good-natured nudge with his elbow. Fay was a bit more sceptical, though.

She looked askance at Roxy and threw out a challenge. "Really? By when, then?"

"This time next week," said Roxy, undeterred for once. Now that she had something to do, and had discovered that she wasn't the only one who might have made the same mistake, she felt that she'd regained some degree of control over the situation. It's high time somebody sorted this out, she determined. If not me, then who? She glanced at Andrew and gave him a thankful smile.

Ian sensed a new lease of energy in her and felt relieved. Maybe – just maybe – this could be her week for turning the corner, just as Andrew had last week.

COMMENTARY: 'THE 3 PILLARS OF PERFORMANCE: ACCOUNTABILITY'

This is the second of 'The Three Pillars of Performance'.

Once we are 'aware', then the role of 'accountability' becomes crucial. In this context, it refers to the link between cause and effect.

We live in a world of cause and effect. Things happen as a result of something that has caused those things to happen. We are where we are now as a cumulative consequence of every decision that we have ever made. Our being aware of the role of cause and effect is what accountability is about.

It is important that we understand and accept our accountability. In many ways, it is the opposite of 'blame'. Blame passes the accountability to someone else, or to something else; it might be the government, the competition, our parents or the Universe. Blame is an interesting concept because it lets us off any accountability that we should bear.

When we blame the traffic for our being late for an appointment, we cop out. The truly accountable truth is that we should have left earlier. We can't do anything about the traffic, but we could have done something about our departure time. Too often, the language we use revolves around blame.

"The market has changed."

"The competition has increased."

"Costs have gone up."

"It isn't very clear."

These are all examples of blame statements. They each have the effect of absolving the speaker or thinker from any accountability.

There may be more truthful and accountable versions of the above situations. Could it be that we were slow to react to the movement of the market? We haven't maintained our competitive advantage? We failed to contain costs? We're unable to understand this?

When we alter our language from blame to accountability, we start to open up to the possibilities of our being able to act differently. When we do something different, we experience different outcomes.

The language of blame implies that the problem, or the cause, is 'out there' and whenever we think the problem is 'out there' we give ourselves an excuse for our not being able to do anything about it.

The attitude of accountability realises that no matter what the situation 'out there' might be, there is always something 'in here' that could change to improve things.

Every minute of the day, we get to choose whether our attitude will be one of blame or one of accountability. Blame is an easy place: it says "it's nothing to do with me; it's someone or something else's fault. I can't do anything about it." No one ever improves with an attitude of blame.

An attitude of accountability is different. Rather, it asks, "What can I do? What is my part in this? How can I adapt my approach? In what way can I change to ensure a different outcome? If what I am doing isn't working, what else can I do that will work?"

That is why accountability is the second of the three pillars of performance. It is about recognising that link between what we do and the results that we get.

The best news about accountability is that it is a choice; once we are aware that it is a choice, it means that our attitude is entirely in our own hands.

Simply, there is no one else to blame.

CHAPTER 15

Ian was still straightening up the chairs in the boardroom for the meeting on Tuesday at twelve when everybody arrived en masse. They were chatting and decidedly noisier than before. He wondered what they'd think of themselves if he showed them footage of what they'd been like on the day of their first 'Tuesday @ 12" meeting.

The one whose demeanour was the most changed this week was Roxy. What a transformation! She was laughing, visibly more relaxed and energetic. Ian hoped that that was a good sign; she'd had a tough time reporting her figures last week. Perhaps she'd managed to claw back that missing four grand somehow.

As it happened, she hadn't. Today was the last meeting of the month, so they were reporting month end figures today, and yes, she'd missed her forecast by four thousand. But there was something that she'd gained from it that would be worth so much more than that in terms of what it could save the company from now on. She'd discovered the 'hole in the system', as Ian had called it last week.

Just as Andrew had taken on the challenge of the 'Who, What, When' the previous week, Roxy had risen to the challenge and committed to getting to the bottom of the mysterious, company 'procedure' regarding off-hire. Today, she had come prepared with her report, and the detective work had given her a real kick.

As usual, Ian started the meeting with Item One on the team's agenda: reporting the results of the 'Who, What, When' of the previous week – completing the accountability loop. He moved straight to Roxy, who seemed eager to share her news.

"We don't actually have a procedure."

Fay couldn't believe her ears. "Oh, come on. Surely there must be one in the Procedures Manual?"

Roxy smiled at her and raised her eyebrows innocently. "Nope – there's nothing there."

Every head turned to Ian with a 'now what?' expression. He looked at them back, with a 'now what?' expression of his own.

Andrew laughed. "Oh, what – I guess that's another 'Who, What, When' challenge, isn't it?"

"What do you think?" Ian smiled. "If so, what's the 'what'?"

Fay responded promptly. "Someone had better write a bloody procedure for 'off-hire', then," she snapped. That reminded Ian: he needed to catch up with Lynne sometime soon. These two were so similar, and they'd both probably flatten him if he ever dared point it out.

"Well, before anybody takes it on from scratch, it's probably smarter in this instance to examine the different procedures we've had in place until now that we discussed last week, decide which one's the most sensible and develop that one for the manual. That way, you won't be writing a brand new procedure from scratch, and you'll be working with one that's already been proven to work even if it hasn't been practiced uniformly yet."

That made sense. Without waiting for anyone to ask the "who's going to do it?" question, Roxy chipped in.

"I'd really like to follow that up," she said, "as I've done a lot of the research on this already. It'd be good to see the task through."

The truth was, she found it satisfying knowing that she was developing a part of the system that neither she nor anybody else could screw up again. She felt more powerful than she ever had in her role, and was even proud of the extra work she was putting in for the company.

What's more, it had given her an insight that had taken her a couple of days to identify: perhaps Lynne wasn't so fool proof herself. After all, if there was no procedure in place in this instance, how many other holes were there in the system? Lynne must feel like she was skating on thin ice, too, at times. It was almost enough to make Roxy feel a bit sorry for her.

Almost.

She gave herself a mental pat on the back. That felt a lot sweeter than her usual brow beating.

In the meantime, the focus of the group had shifted to forecasting the final month end figures . Today, they had the satisfaction of seeing Paul's completed sheet coming together on the wall before their eyes. Two of the departments were going to miss their original forecast: Roxy, who hadn't managed to claw back the four thousand lost on the 'off-hire' mishap, and Natalie, who had missed by just two hundred and thirty pounds.

Still, Andrew could see that for all that, everyone had total clarity and maximum visibility which was inarguably better than the sort of surprise and shock that had always played out in previous end-of-month scenarios with Lynne's haphazard and aggressive leading of the meeting. This way, they all knew where they were and they had a process in place that could only get more robust and dependable. That felt good. The numbers were starting to look better too as the team began to take ownership of them.

Peter from Accounts was happy, too. Together, he and Paul had been surreptitiously checking the reported numbers as the month had worn on to double-check that the figures being reported matched the data that the main accounting system was also reporting. Paul had warned him not to do that forever, as it would undermine the trust that was developing as it smacked of distrust and sneakiness, which Pete had found hilarious.

As for Ian, he was happy for another reason. He could see how the group, with the possible exception of Fay, was really starting to work as one by coming up with its own procedures through discussion, openness and collaboration.

That was no mean feat. This animal had feelings, after all. Significant progress in a short space of time.

COMMENTARY: 'THE 3 PILLARS OF PERFORMANCE: RESPONSIBILITY'

Once we are 'aware' and have chosen an attitude of 'accountability', it befalls us to take 'responsibility' - to decide to take action. This is the third of 'The Three Pillars of Performance'.

In this context, 'responsibility' refers to 'another choice': the choice to act, the choice to change, the choice to do something different.

David Taylor once described coaching as "any and every intervention that enables people, teams and organisations to be their very best." Myles Downey said that "coaching is the series of conversations that help a person perform closer to his potential, understand his role or task, learn what he needs to learn in order to complete his role or task successfully, develop the skills required for the next role, and, on a good day, achieve fulfilment - and maybe a little joy - at work" (*Effective Modern Coaching*, LID Publishing, 2014).

Either way, the output of coaching is for a client to take action of some sort. I believe that responsibility here refers to the choice that we have for our taking action or not.

It is possible for us to be both aware and to be accountable, yet without understanding or acting upon our responsibility to behave in a different way. In that case, nothing is really going to change.

As the well-worn adage tells us, "if you always do what you have always done; you will always get what you have always got."

PART 4

"Nothing in life is more important than the ability to communicate effectively."

GERALD R. FORD, 38th President of the United States of America

CHAPTER 16

Fay fidgeted in her regular place at the end of the table, glancing at the clock every few seconds. Somebody had fixed it. Typical of this lot, she thought – someone always sneaking around and behaving like a creep, trying to look good. The meeting was only five minutes in, and she was itching to say her piece. At least she wouldn't have to wait too long; Ian always started the meeting with follow up on the previous week's 'WWW' forms.

He noticed that she was on edge. What was her problem this time? She was the only one of the group who hadn't entirely bought into the process so far. She was still as scratchy as ever, and while she was clearly intelligent enough to understand that the dynamics between her team members was changing for the better, she didn't seem to appreciate it.

What was it with these Pestons? Perhaps it was just a DNA thing. If that were the case, then he really shouldn't worry that she didn't seem to show much change in her attitude towards the team - or her position, come to that. You need to pick your battles, he reminded himself as he watched her from the corner of his eye while Roxy spoke.

"... so I revisited the 'off-hire' procedure that Andrew mentioned ... the one about stating collection in the agreement prior to delivery of plant equipment, and worked with that. I'd gone through the others pretty thoroughly by that point and this one was easily the most effective and the simplest to use by all of us in the future. I went through it step by step, wrote it all down and have it here as the final document to be added to the Procedures Manual!"

She waved a wad of paper around in uncharacteristic jubilation, and Ian smiled to see her excited and charged for once. What a change from the timid Roxy who'd crept into her chair each meeting so far, dreading her turn to report her department's figures. Good for her.

"Can I say something?" Fay interrupted, and everybody turned to look at her. Here we go, thought Ian. Let's find out what the fuss is about this week.

"I just want to say that it's all very well coming up with a new procedure and all, Roxy," a saccharine smile spread across her mouth, not quite making it to her eyes, "but what about the rest of us?"

"I'm sorry?" Roxy was confused, and fought off the old feeling of inadequacy as it rose from somewhere near her stomach.

"Well, I don't know about anyone else, but I don't remember your asking me what my opinion was on your 'new procedure'."

Fay did little to hide the sniping tone from her voice, and Ian fought the urge to address her on it. There was no place for this sort of mean-spirited behaviour in his meetings, and she should know that by now. The point may be valid but the tone and intention was disrespectful, let alone downright bitchy.

"I ..." Roxy began, blushed bright red and looked at Ian for direction. He stayed silent.

Andrew, who'd been sitting quietly next to Roxy and enjoying her moment of triumph, was incensed. God, that cow. If things didn't improve here after everything they'd learned so far and were beginning to practice as a team together, it would be her fault. Just as rotten as her bloody sister.

He could see that Ian was deliberately staying out of the conversation, and for a moment wondered why. Quickly, he realised that this was an issue for the team to sort out – an 'opportunity' rather than a 'challenge', as they say. Pity that the opportunity hadn't come up outside of the meeting room in private, but still. She'd probably been sitting on this all week, waiting for exactly this public moment before she said anything nasty to Roxy so that nobody could tell her what to do with herself. Well, two could play at that game.

"So, then, Fay, what exactly is it about the procedure Roxy's come up with that doesn't work, would you say?" Andrew copied her smile and challenged her eye to eye from the opposite side of the table, and everyone held their breath.

In mock innocence, Fay held up her hands.

"Just saying, Andrew – surely the setting of a new procedure that's to be carried out by all of us in the future should be decided by all of us before it becomes policy? That's all."

By the look on Andrew's face, it was time for Ian to step in.

"Okay, so if that is an important step," he said, carefully concealing his own opinion, "what would be the steps for establishing a procedure in the future, as a team?" He was tempted to ask Fay directly, but nobody must be put on the spot in this forum. He was here to remove fear, not to encourage it.

Natalie sighed loudly next to Fay. Hadn't all of this been sorted out already? So, they found out last week there was no procedure in place; Roxy wrote one. Sorted, wasn't it? She personally had no gripe with Fay, but she couldn't understand why she'd left it until now to throw a spanner in the works when she could have raised this last week. Besides, it would have saved Roxy a lot of trouble.

"Are we back at Point A again?" she looked around with her hands spread open in disbelief in front of her. Her question was met with a tense silence.

Ian allowed the pause to stretch for a moment, let them feel the change in the atmosphere and to become aware of the disappointment of the sudden halt in progress.

"Not necessarily," he said eventually, with a smile.

Roxy breathed in with relief and waited. She'd worked really hard on this project on top of her usual workload, and she resented Fay's undermining her like this, especially in public. Should she have run it past everyone else first? She could have kicked herself for not thinking of that, but it would have taken so much longer. Who says they'd have all agreed? Fay was the sort of person who'd be awkward every time.

"Talk it out," Ian continued. "Fay, how could Roxy have gone about getting everybody's approval before adding it to the manual?"

"I don't know – like, email it to everyone first?" she sulked. "Call a meeting?"

"Good," said Ian, ignoring her defensiveness and willing the others to do the same.

Andrew wasn't feeling quite so compliant but could see the benefit of their keeping the conversation fair and positive. "And what if you – if someone had disagreed with something? What then? Take a vote?"

This brought Roxy and Natalie into the discussion, each saying that nothing would ever get passed and published at that rate, and so the issue was debated.

Ian sat back and listened, watching them closely. From a classic 'storming' from Fay, the group was starting to 'form' again. With any luck, they'd decide on the way forward in this meeting. 'Norming'. He wished them towards it.

That's just what happened. It might not have been the smoothest debate or even the most effective outcome, but it was theirs; they found it. The best way for them to agree new procedures would be to consult fully on them, debate them fully and only when they have all agreed to commit to them. Then, they should register any changes and additions in the Procedures Manual.

As usual, Natalie wrote it down, and the atmosphere in the room lifted tangibly as they all nodded in agreement. Even Fay couldn't help a small smile of genuine satisfaction. This method would be used every time there was a new procedure to be developed and decided upon. Between them, they decided that when something was 'done' it meant that it had been properly researched, the solution discussed and agreed by all involved, signed off at the appropriate level, registered and filed in the Procedures Manual.

This made the 'WWW' way of instigating changes so much simpler, with everybody now aware of the steps necessary to finalise the changes. Now, Ian wasn't the only one asking "What is the process for ...?": the whole team had learned the power of that very simple question, and they would use it before they pointed the finger at anyone else in the team, looking for a scapegoat.

Andrew felt relieved and drained, in a satisfying way. They were only halfway through this meeting, and look what they'd achieved! It really felt that they were working together as a team – for the very first time.

He caught Ian's eye and nodded his respect. Well handled, he thought.

The 'rhythm' of the meetings was clearly having a good effect on the evolution of the group. Ian was thrilled to see that they were helping themselves to be able to perform better in the future. Their sense of autonomy was growing every week, and it was reflected by each of them individually as well as a whole – even if Fay could be like a hole in the head at times.

By the time they started to discuss the figures, everybody was in a winning mood. The figures themselves were much stronger this month, and as a team they were forecasting £280 000.

"You know what I'm thinking?" Ian said, as Paul wrote the final reported figure down and it was projected onto the wall in full view. He let the ticking of the clock behind him fill the silence, sustaining the new life in the room.

Natalie spoke for all of them. "Could we actually get to £300 000?" She looked around at the others.

They all looked a bit shocked at the thought – it would be the first time they'd cracked such a high figure – but just what if?

Ian let them think about it and waited to see who would ask the key question.

"That's another whole twenty thousand pounds, though," said Roxy, unable to disguise her doubts.

"But what would it take for us to do it?" Natalie wanted to know.

"If you think about it, it's only an extra five thousand per department," shrugged Fay, doodling and thinking hard at the same time.

Ian was taken aback. After her performance earlier, this sort of 'team talk' was unexpected from her. Perhaps this meeting had got through to her on some level – the depths of which could only be known by a Peston … he stifled a laugh and listened to them begin to come up with some ideas on what each of them could do for an extra five thousand pounds.

He knew what he'd like to see added to the LB/NT form this week, after the obligatory "Started and finished on time"; for the first time, it could read "managers started to take the initiative, came up with own ideas on how to take care of their departments. Enjoying taking responsibility."

Things were picking up speed. This seemed to be the appropriate time for him to start to pull back from the meetings.

When they'd finished talking about their new target and how they were going to do it, Ian brought the meeting to close. Before he let them go, though, he threw out one more challenge for them.

"Next week, I'm not going to be here as I've booked myself a short holiday. Which of you will chair the 'Tuesday @ 12' meeting in my place?"

For a moment, they all looked at him in silence. He could see the same question on each of their faces: how are we going to have the meeting without you? It didn't take long for sense to prevail, though, and thanks to the momentum of the last part of the meeting, Andrew wasted no time in speaking up.

"I'll take the meeting next week" he volunteered with confidence. "And I'll email you afterwards, Ian, make sure you have the LB/NT and WWW forms."

"Good man."

Fay started to pack her things. "Going anywhere nice?"

Ian had never understood why people asked that question. As if he would book a holiday somewhere horrible. Still, it was a friendly comment and she meant well by it. That in itself was a victory.

"Off with some mates of mine on a biking trip to Germany," he replied, and couldn't help smiling at the thought. Natalie noticed, and straightened up a little. Who'd have thought? Ian – a biker? She pulled herself up quickly.

She flashed him a quick smile as she followed the others, wishing him well and disappearing from the room altogether, chatting noisily.

For his part, Ian hoped they'd stay that happy for Andrew's sake next week.

CHAPTER 17

"Toasted cheese and tomato ... and a filter coffee," the waitress balanced the tray on her right arm and placed the crockery with care to the side of Ian's laptop as he moved it to make space.

He'd been up since five-thirty, and after the latest "Tuesday @ 12" meeting at Erimus Manufacturing he was more than a little peckish. Still, this would have to do for now. Miriam was making a special, anniversary dinner for the two of them and he was under strict orders to get home by six with a large appetite.

That he would have, he conceded as he bit into nearly half of his sandwich and turned to look out of 'Mimmie's' window onto the pavement outside.

He saw Natalie and Roxy before they entered the coffee shop, chatting and then immediately absorbed in the menu on the long blackboard behind the counter.

It was good to see them out together like this, especially after a shared meeting. It meant that there was more that bound them together after all than just their workplace. He'd never had them down as friends until now. Hopefully, they were beginning to bond, not so much as partners in a rotten regime but as trusted colleagues in a happier, evolving workplace.

The two women placed their orders and looked around for somewhere to sit. They saw Ian straight away. He was hard to miss; he was tall even when he was sitting down, and he'd picked the only sunny spot in the room, next to the window. As he was already smiling at them in greeting and moving his black leather jacket from the chair next to his to accommodate them, they happily joined him at his table.

"Fancy seeing a young thing like you, here," teased Natalie, and Roxy giggled nervously.

Ian greeted them warmly, saved his work and shut the lid of his laptop.

"Good to see you," he returned with a smile. "This makes a change of scene, doesn't it?"

Roxy smiled and removed her scarf, settling down opposite him with Natalie on her left. The meeting today had turned out a lot better than she'd feared. They'd come up with not just a workable plan to finalise future procedures, but they'd set their biggest communal goal yet: £300 000 for the month.

Could they really do it? She wasn't exactly convinced, but she'd left the boardroom that day with a spring in her step and a feeling that everything was going to work out.

On top of all of that, Natalie had asked her to join her for lunch. It was good to have a bit of time with her. She wasn't exactly a girlfriend yet, but hey, who knew? It would make a huge difference to lunchtimes to have somebody to help her window-shop. Middlesbrough had loads to offer, and she hardly ever bothered to explore in the little time she had off.

For her part, Natalie had been surprised to hear herself suddenly ask Roxy to come out with her. She normally just kept herself to herself, but there was something about the camaraderie after the meeting that day that made her suddenly happy, up for a laugh. Roxy could be wishy-washy, but she sensed in her a good heart and possibly a good sense of humour, too.

What the hell, she figured. Out with the old, in with a new way of doing things around here.

So they found themselves quite by accident sitting and chatting with Ian as though he were a pal, and the two of them found the confidence in each other's company to relax, laugh and interrogate him. What was he about? Where did he come from? Did he have family?

Ian answered their questions easily, enjoying their company and happy to see them relaxed. Sometimes the role of 'coach' created a distance between him and his clients that he would rather weren't there. It was natural, he supposed, as he would always come in as the person with all the answers, as far as they were concerned. Of course, he didn't have all the answers: and it wasn't his job to give them answers. It was his job to help them find their own answers, the ones that worked for them. Experience had given him an unshakeable faith in the ability of individuals and groups to find their own best answers. He could help them find the answers, but each situation was completely unique to the team with which he worked.

In this case, they themselves had come up with a way forward for a challenge this morning that would serve them well with many more to come. He wasn't just pleased for them; he was proud of them, too. This team was up against a truly testing range of obstacles. The problem didn't lie only with them by any means.

A fish rots from the head down, he remembered, and made a mental note to use that one day if he needed to with Lynne. Or her father. Whichever pissed him off enough first.

"Andrew is so switched on about his extra five grand for this month. He was already on the phone by the time we left the office," Roxy was saying, leaning across Natalie and taking her jacket potato from the waitress with a thankful smile.

"I know, right? I haven't a clue where I'm going to get mine from yet. I'm putting it out to the Universe, and all that."

Natalie missed Roxy's look of surprise. Was she joking? She was usually so matter-of-fact in meetings that she'd never considered her to have a softer, almost 'bohemian' side.

"Well, you could do a lot worse," Ian said. "Roxy, how did Lynne take your forecast situation for this month?"

Her fork paused precariously between the plate in front of her and her mouth.

"Not particularly well. Then again, I'm still here, which is more than I expected. I wish I knew how to handle her. She really works me up, and even when I know what to say I just can't seem to get the words out properly." Roxy stared at her fork. "She's bullish. As stubborn as one too."

Ian regarded her. "You were asking me about where I grew up," he began. "It wasn't so far from where Lynne grew up, actually."

He had their attention.

"I knew her father from school as we lived in the same village," he wasn't about to reveal which one it was. "A lot of the community was in farming – Angus beef cattle, mostly. The farming kids had long days, what with feeding the calves before school and helping their dads when they went home."

Natalie tried to picture Lynne and Fay doing this, and shook her head.

Ian could see where her imagination was leading her and laughed loudly. "No, not our two heroines," he said, taking a sip of his second cup of coffee. "Earlier than that. But I remember one particular time when I went home from school with a friend of mine who came from a farming family."

Roxy leaned back, making herself comfortable for a good story.

"I remember that we drove up in his mum's car from school and there was a right scene going on in the yard. There were three big men, including my mate's dad, trying to get a heifer into the barn. She wasn't having any of it," he smiled at the memory.

"She dug her feet into the mud and you could see that she'd locked her legs into a brace," he demonstrated with his arms, holding them outstretched in front of him, locked in position. "The more they pulled, the more she pulled back against the rope, and there wasn't a bloody thing any of them could do about it. We wanted to get stuck in, help them out – because of course, two extra pip-squeaks would make the world of difference …"

Roxy and Natalie laughed, picturing the scene.

"… but my friend's mum sent us upstairs to change, first. By the time we came down to the yard, his mum was there, too. She was holding out her hand right in front of the heifer's nose, and we saw it happen right in front of our eyes. The heifer sniffed at her fingers, stuck out the longest black tongue you ever saw, and licked them."

"Gross," muttered Natalie, completely absorbed.

"She moved backwards a couple of steps, and the heifer followed her, sniffing for her fingers again. She kept doing this all the way into the barn – must have been twenty feet – with no fuss. Not so much as a moo."

Roxy tried to figure out the conundrum for herself, but came up with nothing. This was sounding like a parable, or a fable, or something. There had to be a clever answer.

"How did she do that?"

Ian looked at them both, paused for just the right amount of dramatic effect before answering.

"Honey."

Roxy and Natalie looked blankly at him.

"She dipped her fingers in honey that she'd brought out from the kitchen, and the heifer couldn't get enough of the stuff." He laughed, watching their faces.

Natalie was the first to respond. "That's sweet! Typical female intuition."

Roxy was lost in thought.

"I'd better get going," said Ian, putting his laptop in its case and picking up his jacket. "I'll be in touch, and see you both next week."

He nodded at them and smiled, put a generous tip on the table to cover them all and thanked the staff behind the counter as he left the coffee shop.

They watched him leave in silence. After a long pause, Roxy looked at Natalie with a serious expression.

"Do you think he meant that Lynne is the heifer?"

Natalie doubled up, spitting her coffee in hysterics.

CHAPTER 18

It was eleven-thirty on the dot when Carly at the receptionist's desk in Ian's building called him.

"Lynne Peston is here to see you," she said.

He smiled. That was an improvement. Hopefully things would go according to plan in this meeting. He called out, "Come in!" when she knocked and moved to greet her.

She spread her bag, her briefcase and overcoat liberally over the low two-seater and moved over to the chairs at the table in the centre of the room. She looked around her as he chatted amiably and asked her how she liked her tea. There were flyers and a few framed quotes from international business and personal coaches, all with interesting, thought-provoking messages. The light poured in through the floor to ceiling window that overlooked the river, boats and people bobbing about busily in the sunshine under low-flying gulls.

Her office had a massive window just the same; she must get rid of all the junk and old papers in front of it. This was so much more impressive and sort of inspiring.

Ian was saying something about the staff.

"They're really coming along in the meetings, I think. Have you noticed much of a change in the office?

Lynne looked blank and pouted. Shaking her head, she gave a hollow laugh.

"I'm not sure what exactly it is that I'm supposed to be looking for – other than improved performance, that is. And the bottom line is pretty much the same as it was before, from what I can tell. What sort of difference are you talking about?"

"Oh – a willingness to take on more responsibility ... a clearer perception of what everyone else is doing and showing some real initiative. Taking ownership of their part of the business, and ownership of the business's results. Andrew especially seems to be getting a grip of his department and making important decisions these days ..."

"I don't need them to show initiative – I make the decisions. That's the way it always works. I just need them to bloody get on with it."

"Yes ... but every time you make a decision for somebody, you rob them of the opportunity and privilege of learning. They will never get any better and you will always have to make the decisions"

He heard her sigh rudely behind him and focused on the water flow, the steam and the shaft of air that noisily sputtered into the cup. He kept his voice even.

"I meant to ask you. Have you ever done any work to define the core values of the business?."

Lynne snapped her eyes to his back. He shifted, gently preoccupied and relaxed. She gave him the benefit of the doubt.

"Yes. They're in a file somewhere. I'll dig them up and dust them off for you."

Ian drained the teabag from the mug, aimed it at the bin and turned to her. This was going to take more developing than he'd anticipated.

"With every pair of hands comes a free brain, remember," Ian glanced up at her from over his reading glasses.

She laughed. "Oh, please! With that lot?" Her joke seemed to amuse her.

CHAPTER 19

Every Spring, the Tees Valley and its surrounds fairly glitters with an assurance of new life. As everybody in the countryside huddles around log fires and looks forward to warmer days, the gentle hills outside Middlesbrough quietly begin to sparkle and paint fresh colour schemes into the backdrop of a thawing North East. Pale greens, yellows, pinks and blues weave a delicate defence against the last of the winter storms, and everywhere there is a sense of buoyancy and relief.

Everywhere, that is, except in the grounds of the Peston family home. This morning, Michael Peston, having just emerged from a private feedback session in his study with Ian, was bellowing at his daughter.

"For God's sake, Lynne! Keep your leg on! The engine's completely cut out. What do you expect him to do – read your bloody mind? Ride him, for Christ's sake! What's wrong with you?"

He turned to Ian with an exasperated groan and purple cheeks.

"I bloody give up, I do," he spluttered. "How's she going to master that team if she can't master a bloody good horse?" He half-turned back to the manege where Lynne was plodding around in a twenty-metre circle at what she wished were a collected trot.

"I paid damned good money for that beast!" He reverted to yelling again, and Ian ducked involuntarily.

He wished Michael would give up, frankly. Regardless of how annoying Lynne could be, she must be dying inside. The easiest thing for her might be for Ian to leave, save her from his witnessing this latest patriarchal put-down. But he was there now, and it might be even more embarrassing for her if he left out of obvious pity. So he lingered, with his hands in his pockets and pursing his lips to stop himself from giving Michael a piece of his mind.

What Michael didn't know was that Ian had been watching her from his position inside the study.

He hadn't recognised her at first. He saw a horse and rider working well together, firstly on simple schooling moves – a collected walk, to halt, to working trot on a serpentine, back to a collected walk, to halt and rein back. Then the same sequence on the other rein. It was only as she briefly readjusted her hat that he realised who the rider was.

From then, he'd had to concentrate hard on what Michael was saying to stop himself from watching them. Horse and rider worked together as one. Her aids were subtle, her hands still, and although she was undeniably a large lass she looked as though she were floating. The best thing of all, he realised with a jolt - she was smiling.

As she moved the immaculate grey gelding into a series of more complicated half-passes diagonally across the school, a light came on in his mind. How could she have such empathy with this beautiful animal and yet offer none to her team at work?

Together, they were a sight for sore eyes. Mesmerising.

It was only when he and Michael had gone outside to watch her that it all went tits up. Damn the man. He always had been a prize asshole.

Now, Lynne was struggling to communicate at all with her horse, and he was playing up. The more he tossed his head and resisted her leg aids, the more frustrated she became, all under the critical eye of her father. She was getting rattled, and soon the old Lynne that Ian had come to know at her workplace was back in full force.

"Come on, you bastard!" she yelled, using her schooling whip on the grey's sensitive shoulder. He bucked in answer and nearly unseated her.

"Screw this, I'm going," Michael eventually said to Ian's relief. "Bloody get yourself sorted out or I'll get my money back!" he shouted over his shoulder as he strode back into the house.

Ian watched him leave and turned back to Lynne, now circling in a passable, collected walk.

She took her time, now, Ian noted: halted and reined back, making him stand square and quiet. Finally, she patted him, running her hand up his mane and praising him softly to end their time together on a good note. Regardless of how badly things had gone, she would never let her horse leave a schooling session thinking that he'd let her down.

She dismounted, red in the face, running up her stirrups like a robot and taking the reins, fairly dragging the grey behind her to the entrance of the school and giving Ian a curt nod.

"That's a beautiful horse," said Ian quietly, reaching to touch the velvety muzzle. He was rewarded with a gentle whiffle and a slow movement of his jaws on the bit, showing that he was relaxing.

Lynne moved her right arm protectively under his neck and tickled him behind his ear.

"Too good for me," she said with regret, and again, Ian was surprised. He warmed to her immediately. She loved this horse.

"What is he – sixteen three, seventeen hands?"

It was Lynne's turn to be surprised. "Seventeen, yes. You know horses? Fury, meet Ian," she said, patting the horse on the neck with a little smile.

"'Fury'? His name's 'Fury'?"

"Well, 'Snowland of Fury', to give him his full title," she murmured, focused on her horse and completely missing Ian's touch of irony.

He couldn't help grinning as he walked with them both to the stables, set out in an expensive, modern American barn fashion that appealed to him. Everything neat, clean, accessible, airy and light. Just as the office should be, he thought.

"I was watching you earlier," he ventured, feeling his way carefully to open a conversation that his instinct told him she'd be interested in. "You had him going really well for you."

"Yeah? Well, tell Dad that," she grumbled, sliding open the stall door and letting her horse walk in on his own. She followed him in and started to untack.

"No, really. You did. You're a natural. You're empathic. He loved working with you when you asked him to."

Lynne busied herself with the girth, hiding the flush of pleasure that crept onto her face. It was true: Fury would do anything she asked of him. The moment she'd demanded he do something was the moment he'd become confused, insecure with her and unsure of what she wanted. She knew that, but it was so hard under her father's scrutiny and criticism.

"What are your plans for him? He'd make a great hunter."

"Actually, he jumps like a stag," she said, suddenly animated. "I had him out the other day and he took a four bar with ease. I'm hoping to compete with him one day – maybe next summer - but I'm the one who's out of shape." She stopped suddenly, biting her lip and berating herself for giving herself away.

Ian snatched the opportunity to keep the conversation flowing, allow her to follow her interest.

"Do you have a plan?"

"What do you mean, 'a plan'?" asked Lynne, turning to him with the saddle in her arms.

"A daily, weekly, monthly plan that you can work to – you know, for him. One small goal at a time. Written down, so that you can track his progress," he picked his words carefully.

"No – I don't. But that's not a bad idea." Lynne looked around her. "I could do something like that and put it on the wall – up there, opposite his stall maybe ..."

Her tone had completely changed, Ian noticed. She was speaking with sudden interest, almost excitement.

"Yes, so he can read it when you're not around."

She laughed, a genuine, happy laugh that threw her head back.

"He's a winner in the making, that one. Dad wouldn't like it much, though. He'd say it was distracting me from work, or something."

"Does your dad have to know?"

She looked at him and a smile slowly lit up her face. She was really very attractive when she was allowed to be.

He smiled back. "I used to jump a bit myself," he said. "I'd be keen to see what you come up with, see how you two get on."

She nodded, sliding the barn door closed.

"I'd like that. A lot. Thanks, Ian." She flashed a wide grin at him and shoved the saddle at him to carry.

He laughed and took it happily. He watched her walk in front of him and when he was sure she wouldn't see, looked back at Fury who had his nose buried deep in his hay rack.

"Thank you," he whispered.

CHAPTER 20

This was heaven. Keeping right instead of left was a new challenge in itself.

This particular route had been opened in 2004, and it was the first time Ian and his biking buddies were tackling it. A thousand kilometres of some of the most picturesque towns, villages and mountains in Germany, and a whole week to conquer it.

He hadn't had this much fun in twenty-five years. They'd ridden together for all of that time, enjoying a natural, easy friendship that can only happen between those who've misspent their youth together.

There was a lot to be said for old bonds and best kept secrets.

Directly ahead of him, Graeme was riding like a god on his Italian sports bike. God knew how many flies were squashed already onto its front. He wouldn't let anybody near enough to his beloved bike to check, in any case.

From his position at the rear this morning, Ian could watch his closest friends enjoy themselves in the surroundings that were positively overwhelming him. From hour to hour, they rode through mountainside villages, tore down open roads and stopped off for snacks on riverbanks.

This was living. He focused on his being here, right now, in the moment, with his friends ahead of him embracing it all, too.

He noticed Graeme suddenly point to something on his right, and he turned to see five horses running together next to a fence, racing the bikers. For some reason he thought of the team at Erimus Manufacturing, and before he knew it, he was analysing everything again.

If that bunch were here they'd be all over the road.

Whether it's a corporate team, a family or just a gaggle of hairy bikers on a short biking trip, the 'four stages of grouping' is never a linear process. Norming could overtake Performing, and before you knew it, you'd be back with Storming charging ahead again. The dynamic would change frequently.

His hand twitched at the thought of having his turn up at the front, but he stayed in place, happy to observe in this reflective part of his ride.

He wished he could switch off from the constant commentary in his head about how much this trip reflected the core values, group dynamics and underlying psychology of his work. It was like listening to background, tin-pot commercial radio on a dodgy frequency.

Looking up through his visor at the clear sky, he muttered, "Can't a bloke catch a break?"

He sent the complaint out there, into the wind as it tore past him, towards the sun as it had started to turn from bright yellow to burnished gold beyond the vineyards that flanked him.

Immediately, he took it back and smiled, his cheeks touching the inside of his helmet. His view on everything around him was unforgettable. He wouldn't change where he was for the world.

Before he'd left the Erimus Manufacturing offices, the atmosphere had been more fun and positive than ever. Well, at least since he'd met them, which he felt he could safely assume was the same thing. At the end of the seventh meeting, Ian had put it straight to them.

"How do you feel about work right now?"

Everybody smiled.

"Loving it!"

"We're definitely moving forward."

"We have control at last!" This last response came from Fay as she raised her arms and punched her fists in the air, making everyone laugh.

"Go on, then, Natalie – how would you say the group's moved forward?" Ian encouraged her share some good news with the others. He noticed as they all leaned in a little to hear what she had to say.

"Oh – the difference is huge. Since I've been keeping the LB/NT forms, I've been able to see how things that we once thought were a bit strange for us we now do as a matter of course. Every week, I know that I can write 'started and finished the meeting on time', for example. None of my staff ever bother me with anything around lunchtime on Tuesdays, now. They all know I'm busy and somehow, they've helped themselves to get on with tasks without constantly asking me for directions."

Andrew nodded. His own team had given him the same space on Tuesdays, and it freed him up to focus on the business rather than working in the business and get ahead.

"I have the chance to think about what we need to achieve from our time together instead of arriving at the meeting unprepared," he said. "It means that I always have something to contribute to our discussion. That makes me feel like I have some autonomy in my job – it makes everything more worth the effort, somehow."

Ian was glad. It was true that several important issues had been raised recently with this extra degree of foresight.

"I don't think we should ever skip a 'Tuesday @ 12' meeting from now on. It's so much better knowing what each other is doing, what our purpose is as a team." Natalie hit the nail on the head in her usual, straight-talking style.

Ian took it as confirmation that things were going in the right direction before he sent out his handover email to the group.

"Dear All,

This is to confirm that I will be on leave as of the end of this week and won't be back in the office until the Tuesday after next.

Next Tuesday, Andrew will chair our regular 'Tuesday @ 12' meeting in my absence.

Bring with you your figures, departmental reports and, of course, any issues, concerns or praise you have noted over the past week. Particularly the latter!

I look forward to receiving your 'Liked Best/Next Time' report for the week, along with any 'WWW' that may arise in the meeting.

If you have any concern that may have sprung up over the last week, please take seriously my full encouragement to raise it in the next meeting while the issue is fresh. Together, you have all the skill and ability that you need to solve any problem that may arise. Nip it in the bud, as you are used to doing by now. Natalie has agreed to document everything as usual and send it to me while I am on leave so that I can keep abreast of your progress.

Looking forward to catching up with you the week after next!

To your success,

Ian."

He was never supposed to have been there for longer than one month. Initially, that had been the agreement he'd made with Michael. Things had evolved differently, though; the team itself had evolved.

He thought back to the evening he spent with the Pestons for dinner two months ago. If anyone asked him then why he'd taken this job on, he wouldn't have had an answer.

Now, though, he knew. The team didn't deserve to be terrorised all the time. They didn't deserve to be constantly fearful and threatened. They were capable of performing at a far higher level and of being happier, if they were just allowed to be.

They say when one teaches, two learn. The art of teaching will always be a two-way process and in taking on this assignment Ian had had to learn patience. Over the course of the last several weeks, he had become more tolerant. More adept at being firm rather than dictatorial. He'd learned an invaluable life lesson himself.

Had he not been patient, he might very easily have missed the best opportunities to help the team rise to their next level. What if Andrew hadn't been the one to stand up and volunteer to take over the meeting this week? What if he hadn't been there to witness Lynne's great horsemanship?

What if Roxy hadn't had to change her forecast and given herself permission to deal with the reality of the situation? What if they hadn't discovered the holes their lack of process was creating for them?

Decisions are made, actions are taken ... and you must ride it all out. It takes patience, self-control and flexibility to see the opportunities and use them when they come up.

Some people might call it luck, or Fate, he reasoned. He considered the accident on the workshop floor, and Andrew's heavy sense of guilt concerning it.

But much of the situation, accidents, lack of process, lack of communication were really the consequences of a less obviously identifiable culprit: these were all symptoms of the culture of the company, Ian knew. the less people cared, for each other, for the business, for the results, the more things like this would happen. Not for the first time, he wondered about the company's core values.

Up ahead, Ross signalled to let Graeme overtake him for a while. Ian looked in his mirror and prepared to overtake soon.

The last time they'd taken a tour in Germany together they were younger, fitter and a hell of a lot noisier. Ian could remember vividly tearing through the main street of a little village, his mates behind him as he blazed the trail past a post office, the village shop and a little old lady as she took her daily stroll back home from the greengrocer's.

As he cruised past her with his mates behind him, he cut his engine so that it continued turning over. At the right moment, he gave it the gas and it took with a loud bang, scaring the life out of the little old lady and scattering her groceries all over the pavement. Great fun, back then ... but naturally, not any more.

These days, his biking buddies weren't up for that stuff, as every one of them had grown up – become somebody new. They all had careers, families, responsibilities. As a group of riders today, they were totally different to the group they'd been as they tore up the villages back in the Eighties.

Now their core values were evident in the way they behaved, as they are with every community. They still valued the fun and freedom that riding high powered motorbikes gave them and at the same time they valued their safety and the responsibility they all had in their jobs and the community. How this manifests is an unspoken thing - a shared ethic – just something that happened naturally between them. They shared the same values, so rules were never laid down, per se. Nobody had ever stood up and read out a list of commandments before they rode: it's just a given. Understood. Logical, quite apart from sensible.

For example, the rider who knows the roads, leads on the roads. The second fastest rider always rides at the back, as you don't want anyone riding faster than his ability in an attempt to keep up. If you're never the last, you never have to do that. When turning, somebody waits at the corner to make sure that nobody gets lost. That way they can be as safe as possible whilst riding at a decent pace.

A few months ago, another biker had joined them for a ride. They had no problem with that, but this lad didn't 'get it'. He didn't share their core values. It was embarrassingly clear from his behaviour within the first ten minutes of the ride.

He tried several times to coerce them into racing, swerved dangerously in between the other vehicles on the road and generally behaved like a git. When he tore away from a standstill at the third set of traffic lights, Ian's group merely let him go and changed their route. He was last seen disappearing over the brow of the hill.

He laughed as he remembered. Poor sucker. He who doesn't

'get it' has to go. He was ejected as a healthy organ would eject a harmful virus.

Core values. They determine behaviour.

And frightening the wits out of little old German ladies wasn't one of them, not any more, he told himself firmly as he accelerated, overtaking Ross to catch up with Graeme.

It felt great to be alive.

COMMENTARY: 'CORE VALUES'

We are all driven by a whole raft of values and beliefs. They lie deep within the identity of each of us. Mostly, they are unconscious facets of an individual's personality and motivations.

Beliefs are things which we hold to be true, while values are things that we hold to be important. Nancy Kline describes values as 'the unconscious filters that drive our behaviour'. We make decisions based on our own individual values, which tend to sit in hierarchies. To illustrate, two people may share the same highest values but if they are in a different order then those two individuals will probably respond behave differently to the same stimulus.

Every group of people, formal or informal, permanent or temporary will have their own specific 'Core Values'. Those core values will probably not be explicit but they will be evident in the behaviour of the group. Just as our individual values are the unconscious filters that drive our behaviour, so core values drive the behaviour of the group. They dictate what is acceptable and what is unacceptable behaviour, and they are the result of the aggregate of the values of the most influential members of the group.

Defining core values is an extremely important part of understanding what drives and motivates any group. However, they usually exist on a subconscious level and are implicit rather than explicit. Because they are implicit, they are susceptible to change, for the better or worse without any conscious decision. This makes them potentially fickle and ephemeral.

The very best and most enduring organisations realise the significance of Core Values and seek to codify them so that they can be monitored and maintained in a more constant manner.

As I said, all groups, communities and collections of people will have Core Values, which will unconsciously drive their behaviour and if you know what you are looking for it is easy to see those core values in action in that group.

I can quite easily see the Core Values of my biking buddies at play every time we go out. We all like to press on a bit - which is why we ride motorbikes, after all - but we are also all of an age with families, businesses and loved ones. Those two values of speed and safety are evident in the way we behave.

We have never really spoken about this; it just sort of happens quite naturally. Wherever we happen to be, the guy that knows the area best takes the lead, or the one with the Sat Nav or who has done the most research. Why? He is the one can ride most quickly, most safely.

As a troupe, we all obey that unwritten rule. The second quickest rider will take up the rear, to make sure that no one is worried about being left behind. Often, the most dangerous thing when riding as a group is for someone to be riding faster than his or her capabilities for fear of being left behind and getting lost. When we come to a T junction or a turn off, the second rider will stop, wait and indicate the direction for the others making sure they all go the right way, until the 'rear gunner' comes along ensuring that everyone is going in the right direction.

None of these behaviours is formal, rehearsed or planned. They arise naturally as a manifestation of those core values. We look after each other. We care about each other in a way that can often only easily arise when we are all involved in something that is intrinsically dangerous.

When someone joins our group who doesn't share our core values, it's interesting to see how we react. He may be riding badly or dangerously, too fast or too slow; our group will do its best to eject this outsider like a healthy organ will reject a virus in an unconscious act of self-preservation. We will either leave the interloper behind or let him go on ahead as though we had pre-planned the preservation of safety, speed and care - our unspoken core values.

Successful organisations have realised that if they codify their core values they can preserve them, and even scale them as the organisation scales.

CHAPTER 21

Andrew made his way through the open plan office area and straight to the staircase that led to the boardroom upstairs. He had a collection of reporters' notepads and pens, and he bounded up the stairs to start putting them out for the others in good time for this week's 'Tuesday @ 12' meeting.

He was excited. This time, he was going to chair it, and although it was only his close colleagues who were going to be present he had butterflies in his stomach. Fortunately, they weren't the 'crippling fear' variety; rather, they were the 'supercharged, on track, let's kick some butt and go' type, and he was looking forward to the others' arrival for their very first time together as a team, with no outside help.

He'd spent a lot of time preparing for this meeting. A couple of days earlier, he'd booked out the boardroom so that he could practice standing in Ian's usual spot and speaking to the room.

It was then that he'd noticed the walls. He'd already fixed that nerve-splitting light, but now, standing here in the position of somebody who wanted to run a meeting that had a lasting, positive effect on everyone present, he realised how dead the room was. How was anyone supposed to feel energised or come up with creative ideas in an environment that looked like it had been used as an army base?

He'd called Roxy. She was good at this sort of thing.

"Well, what sort of atmosphere do you want to create in there?" she'd asked, clenching her mobile between her shoulder and chin as she expertly chopped parsley for sprinkling on a new chicken dish she was trying out.

"You know – sort of business-like, but uplifting ..." Andrew was out of his depth.

"Yes – a sort of energising theme with an accent wall, maybe," she sounded like she had something in her mouth.

"What's an accent wall?" Andrew whimpered, wondering if he should have called Pete instead.

She'd really come through for him, though. Together, they'd discovered tins of 'Parchment' paint in the storage area behind reception: a muted, yellowy-cream – enough to cover three of the four walls and lighten the place considerably, tying in the wood-effect of the table and make sense of the furniture a whole. Roxy had added her touch with a blast of 'Burnt Cerise', which made Andrew's head hurt when he saw it in the tin, but drew the whole room together in designer-style.

Between the two of them and two members of the sales team who were sworn to secrecy and treated to lunch as a 'thank you', they'd resurrected the boardroom.

As he looked around him now, it looked like a dream. It stank of new paint, but Fay would be the only one to ever dare mention it, he was sure. Just imagine what it will look like when we have awards on those walls, he thought, as he straightened up the chairs and flicked imaginary dust off the clock.

By a quarter to twelve, the room was ready with pads of paper and pens in position as Ian would have liked. It was a proper boardroom, ready for a proper meeting.

At ten to twelve, Pete from Accounts came in with his laptop and a brand new projector screen. He whistled at the transformation.

"Thought we might edge a little closer to the twenty-first century this week," he joked, handing Andrew the cable. He switched on his laptop, waited for the image of his desktop to appear on the screen and opened the correct folder for that week's figures.

Lynne wouldn't recognise any of this, Andrew told himself with satisfaction. We've come a long way since those old times, when all that happened in the irregular meetings was a fresh sacrifice of another colleague.

He started watching the clock at five to twelve, and suddenly realised how Ian must have felt every week, not knowing if his charges would bother to pitch up on time. Andrew really hoped that they would: what if they figured that he wasn't as important to impress with good time-keeping as Ian, and dawdled along until ten past? That was just the sort of thing Fay would do. He wouldn't put it past her.

He had nothing to worry about, though. Far from dawdling, Fay was the first one in, closely followed by Roxy and Natalie.

That was the sum of their group, today, and they were overawed at the change in their usual meeting place.

"Look at us – the A Team! Brilliant work, you two!" Natalie laughed.

"It's down to just the five of us, now. Well, until Lynne comes back in, I suppose," Fay characteristically dampened the mood in the room without so much as turning a hair.

The idea of Lynne's being back in their midst, disturbing the happy ambience and threatening to derail the team after all this effort was enough to depress them all. Andrew had a brief vision of sparks flying, people storming out, papers being torn and stopped himself.

That wasn't happening right now. It probably never would happen, either. Right now, he had his colleagues with him in a room full of opportunity for a full hour. He also had a way forward to chair the meeting and see what could be achieved by the end of it. Right here, right now, this moment is what matters, he told himself firmly, and addressed everybody formally.

"Thanks for coming, everyone," he said, "and Natalie, the first entry in the 'Liked Best' column of our LB/NT should be - "

"Meeting started on time!" they all chanted together, and burst out laughing.

Andrew smiled, breathed in happily and relaxed. They were off to a good start.

As the hour wore on, the group turned its attention to the figures. They were on the third week of the month, and, so far, everybody was holding to their original department forecasts. However, last week they'd had a team lightbulb moment, and had decided that they should increase the target by twenty thousand to reach their record of £300 000 for the month.

If anyone thought now that maybe that decision had been a little rash, they weren't going to admit it. It meant that each department needed to increase its forecast by five thousand.

"When you put it like that, it doesn't sound like very much at all," commented Fay, and everyone agreed with her. "Has anybody done it yet?"

Nobody had, but that wasn't surprising.

"Does everyone have some ideas by now about how they might generate it, at least?" asked Andrew, and went around the table inviting them each to share their suggestions. In that conversation, he noticed, the tone was respectful and more besides: they were keen to help each other – think outside of their own worlds and see what could be done as a whole.

Why did they suddenly seem like completely different people to the boring, aggressive idiots he thought he'd landed himself with when he started here six months ago? Had they changed, or had he changed?

He wanted to understand this better. There was so much that he wanted to ask Ian – how did he seem to guess how people are going to behave? How has he motivated these results from a team that once gave the word 'dysfunctional' a whole new meaning?

He wondered if he'd ever have a good enough reason to get some coaching of his own with Ian. He was feeling a responsibility towards his department, his team, and for the first time, to Erimus Manufacturing as an entity.

Wow. Forget coaching with Ian: maybe he needed a shrink instead.

He was in the middle of these plans when Natalie spoke up.

"By the way," she said, once the subject of the figures was finished, "may I raise something with the group that might need the treatment of our brand new 'Procedure' procedure?"

Roxy laughed, but Andrew looked at Natalie seriously, his butterflies beginning to start dancing again.

"I was discussing a contract with a brand new client on Friday – could be signed off revenue for about six thousand every month for the next two years and it would be great to get the agreement. Before he would officially sign though, he wanted to confirm our terms and conditions. So, I referred him to the website as usual ..."

"It says on the contract, 'For full terms and conditions visit the website'," said Fay irritably. What was wrong with her? She knew that well enough.

"Yes, but he pointed out that there are no terms and conditions on the website."

Fay went white and shut up suddenly.

"Pete," said Andrew, indicating his laptop, "could you please go to the terms and conditions page of our website?"

Pete was already on it, scrolling to the bottom of Erimus Manufacturing's Homepage to the t's and c's link in small text. He clicked the link and everybody looked up at the screen to see.

It was a curious blurb of Latin, probably a bit of Greek thrown in – just random text to show that the page was supposed to exist.

The trouble was, as Natalie's client had so rightly pointed out, there was no information there, and before he signed anything he wanted to be sure precisely what he was signing up to, thank you very much.

Andrew turned back to his colleagues. "Does anybody know anything about this?"

Fay looked as though she were about to explode. "Bloody hell, that little rat!" she spat, and Andrew frowned at her.

"It's bloody Sean's fault. I told him at least four weeks ago that I wanted those Terms and Conditions altered and he's had the amendments ever since. All he had to do was amend the content on the page and reload it! I'll bloody kill him!"

She grabbed her diary and started to write in it furiously.

Roxy looked up at Andrew, confused. Natalie raised her eyebrows and looked at Andrew, too. So did Pete, with his eyes as wide as saucers.

"Fay, Sean left the company three weeks ago. Remember?"

Remember? Remember what? "I didn't receive any letter of resignation," she mumbled, turning white once more.

Andrew couldn't believe what he was hearing.

"Lynne fired – I mean, let him go," he quickly corrected himself. "Didn't you know?"

This was incredible. By far the juiciest, most dramatic thing that had happened while he had been with the company. Now, though, it gave him no vengeful satisfaction whatsoever. This was potentially huge for the morale of the team, and had already affected God knows how many accounts.

Fay looked around the table, stunned. She looked really upset this time, Roxy thought. Almost like she was going to cry. Don't do that, whatever you do! She willed her to stay together, and felt genuinely sorry for her. Her sister had completely undermined her.

"How could she do that?" Fay spoke under her breath, almost to herself. She remembered where she was and spoke from the heart. "Natalie, everyone – I am so, so sorry. I didn't even know that Sean wasn't here. I didn't notice. I'm Head of this Branch and he was my responsibility, not Lynne's. How could I not notice he was gone?"

Natalie stretched her arm out and put it around her colleague's shoulders in spontaneous, heartfelt gesture. She hadn't been expecting this. Nobody had. She'd never seen Fay humble, remorseful or anything remotely like it.

She looked up at Andrew for the next instruction.

His butterflies had turned into hammers. This was going to take some sorting out ... but at least they had the 'Procedure' procedure to help them get there. He suggested that he and Fay meet later that day to discuss what had happened, give her a chance to collect herself, and tried to end the meeting on time on a positive note with the LB/NT form.

There was always something to like best, after all.

Personally, what he liked best was that he had his one big reason to ask Ian for private coaching: somebody had to create a proper process around here for managing people and that should include conducting regular appraisals. What had happened to Sean wouldn't happen to anyone else from now on.

He made that decision, right in the moment, there and then.

PART 5

"Education is the most powerful weapon which you can use to change the world."

NELSON MANDELA, first democratically voted President of the Republic of South Africa

CHAPTER 22

Ian was handed a cup of tea by Katie, his P.A., at his light, airy office in Stockton. He was making notes on the one-to-one meeting he'd just had with Andrew, focusing on how they should take their time together forward.

Erimus Manufacturing had made him change in a way he hadn't anticipated: he'd had to become more patient. In a previous life as an MD, he'd run so many meetings with a tough hand, a distinct leadership style that suited him but possibly few others, when he reflected on it.

That was one of the reasons why he'd embarked on his own journey of discovery: what made people want to do their best? What made him want to do his best? He could see that in his past, he had tended to dominate meetings, and it made him wonder today how many people he may have unwittingly discouraged.

It wasn't a comfortable thought.

Andrew was off to a good start, though: he listened well and asked the right questions. That afternoon, he'd had another 'Eureka' moment.

For Andrew, it had felt decidedly weird walking into Ian's office instead of having Ian visit them at Erimus Manufacturing, but not at all unpleasant. He'd taken an afternoon's leave to have this time with him in what he hoped would be straight-to-the-heart, mind-blowingly awesome coaching, one to one.

Of course, he was open-minded and not at all sure what to expect, but he was excited. Things had started to change for the better at Erimus; anybody who knew the company would see that.

One thing the development of the team had done, mind you, was widen the gap between Lynne and the management team. It felt like there were two distinct cultures in one business, and they were hardly complementary. The one felt like a prison system, the other like a dynamic, evolving business that was beginning to turn heads and gain a great reputation.

Andrew wanted to know how it had become this way, but mostly, what he could do to change it so that they were all pulling in the same direction.

He stirred his tea thoughtfully as he waited for Ian to join him, looking out of the large window over the River Tees, the sun glimmering on the water.

"Andrew! Great to see you!" Ian burst into his thoughts with a happy, tanned and welcoming face. "What a pleasure to see you here. Now – do you have to get back to the office or onto a meeting later, or are you okay for time? Best that I know up front."

Andrew shook his head with a smile. "I've taken the afternoon off."

Well, that showed commitment to the process, Ian thought, and settled himself down to discuss why Andrew was there.

"Things are starting to work better at the office," he said, not knowing quite where to begin, "but there are some gaps that are posing problems – big ones, I think – and I really want to see them sorted out. I know it's not my place to do that or anything ..."

Ian pictured Lynne's face as she found out that he'd been coaching Andrew on the quiet. Let's not go there, he thought.

"... but I want to know for myself, not just for Erimus. I want to learn how to start getting people to work together. What's the secret?"

Ian burst out laughing. "There's no secret. It's a case of their wanting to do something rather than making them do something. Is that what you're talking about?"

Andrew nodded. "That and other things. When Sean was fired, it was really unfair. He had no idea it was coming. He thought he was doing a good job. There had been no discussion about his performance or the need for him to change. He was completely blindsided. That can't be right. That can't be fair. There isn't even an appraisal system in place to speak of, which there should be as a matter of urgency. I don't want to see anybody else 'let go', as Lynne put it, unfairly again. There's a way of doing it right."

His phone buzzed and started to move across the round desk in front of them, and he leaned over to see who the incoming call was from.

"Ah. Ian, would you mind if I take this quickly? It's Sam from the workshop."

"By all means, go ahead," Ian waited. He'd expected Andrew to have switched it off before they started their meeting, and Ian was surprised he hadn't. but that in itself presented an opportunity and Ian was interested to see why he was taking work calls on his afternoon off.

Andrew took the call where he sat, listening to Sam for about a minute and then giving him instructions on how to follow up a recent email from a client.

"So is an appraisal system is something you'd like to know more about? Ian asked. when Andrew had finished with the call.

"I think so" Andrew replied, and when I understand it I would like to develop a system for us at Erimus and roll it out as soon as possible.

"We should take it one step back from that point and talk about the recruitment procedure, too, in that case." Ian suggested.

Andrew wrote it down and agreed; it made sense.

"Recruitment is a complex area Andrew, but one of the major considerations is finding people who align with the company at a values level. If you employ someone who naturally shares your company's core values, you'll have a staff member who's in it for the long haul. Who believes what you believe and acts the way the very best of the company acts, without being told"

That was interesting. Andrew sat up.

"I don't know what our core values are. Nobody seems to."

"Well, believe me, your core values will be evident if you care to look. Every community operates to their own set of core values." Ian said remembering how obvious his biking buddies core values were to the interested observer. "Whether they are written down or not" Ian said. "Simply, they will be the aggregate of the personal values of everybody on the team. Unless those values are codified, written down and defined, though, they'll change as the personnel changes. A strong character can influence the community's core values for the better or the worse. If, on the other hand, they are explicit, we can manage them, preserve them and scale them. We can recruit with them in mind, and as long as the recruitment process is working well, everybody should be on the same page as far as the culture goes."

Andrew looked thoughtful. "We're not that, by a long way. Can people change? Adopt them – once we know what they are, of course?"

Ian shook his head. "Core values are not a cloak that you throw around your shoulders before you come to work. If one of your core values is Honesty, for example, a dishonest person will not be able to be honest during office hours just to satisfy the core values. Sooner or later, his true nature will show through. It's about 'who we are'. Remember what Gandhi said: 'A person cannot do right in one department of life while attempting to do wrong in another department.

Life is one indivisible whole.'"

"Then there's Lynne herself," Andrew said with a sigh. Ian smiled at his train of thought. "I can see where she's going wrong sometimes – she's so aggressive with her staff, especially in meetings. We're all dreading the day she rejoins us, I think. How do I 'manage the manager'?" he frowned. "If I could find a way to encourage her in the right direction, I wouldn't have to bite my tongue so often."

Of course, Ian was fully aware of the friction between Lynne and the managers, and particularly between her and Andrew as he was getting to know him quite well. It wasn't a power struggle, exactly; it was more that their personalities were very different. Their values and beliefs, particularly about how to treat people were wildly different. Lynne was volatile and explosive, while Andrew was measured, delighting in things being done 'right'.

"That can be tricky," Ian remarked, "as you have to answer to her ultimately. 'Managing up', as it's called, requires skill, courage and judgement in equal measure."

Andrew nodded.

"But there is no reason why you, and the rest of the team can't develop the skills to do that."

Andrew pulled a face, at the thought of the task.

His phone buzzed again. This time, it was a text message.

"Sorry," he reached forward to pick it up and deftly texted a short message back.

Ian raised an eyebrow. "Trouble?"

"That was Barbara wanting to know which code to use for a credit note," he returned the phone to the desk once more.

Ian stood up and looked for a book on 'core values' that he could lend Andrew.

"Tell me – does your team always call you this frequently? Even on your day off?"

Andrew was taken aback.

"This is normal. They like to get things right, my lot," he grinned.

Ian moved back to the table and placed the book on it.

"I see. Are you their 'Rescuer'?"

Andrew looked disconcerted for a second and slowly smiled. "Some people just aren't capable of thinking for themselves, I guess. I reckon if I keep showing them, the penny will finally drop."

Ian put his head to one side; now he knew where to start Andrew's own development process.

"Tell me", he began "what sort of people do you have on your team? Are they capable, competent, intelligent"?

"Well, yes ... for the most part," Andrew muttered, not knowing where this might go.

"Do they have full lives? Children, families, dependants, mortgages? Car finance, life insurance and pension funds?"

"All of them do." He still wasn't sure what Ian was driving at.

Ian smiled now, too. "So, what you are telling me is that they are all perfectly capable of thinking for themselves, apart from the eight hours they spend with you every day , when you have to make every decision for them ...?"

Andrew leant back in his chair and laughed. He'd never thought of it that way. Ian was right. They needed their autonomy, too.

"Spot on," he said, and finally switched off his phone.

At last, Ian thought. He's seen the light.

"How we deal with people is always dependent on how we perceive them. If you perceive your team to be numbskulls, you'll treat them as though they are. Here's how I think we could loosely plan our sessions so that you get the most from our time together. We'll talk about core values," he wrote it down in his file, "and the process of recruitment – have you heard of the 'A-Player Grid'?"

Andrew shook his head.

"Then we'll focus on that next time," Ian said, continuing to write, "and that will lead us to your being able to develop an appraisal system for your own team that you might then roll out to the rest of the company. You have to be able to measure somebody's performance based on their core values. If they're not a fit, they need to go. Sometimes you can have a member of the team who's getting great results, but who doesn't get what the company's really about – who you are as a team. I know a few really good salespeople who have been exited from organisations I have been responsible for as a result."

Andrew felt unsettled. This was a lot to take in and it sounded more brutal than he'd expected. He thought of Dave, his foreman, who was good at has job but who seemed to be just there for his pay packet. He didn't seem to get what Erimus were all about. He didn't talk with the rest of the team and seemed to be the only one who wasn't buying into the newfound sense of direction that everyone else had. Guess he's a 'C-Player', he thought, and winced at the thought of exiting him.

"Are you telling me that I need to get rid of a high performer simply because he doesn't behave the way I'd like him to?"

"Yes. That is precisely what I am saying – unless, of course, you value that one individual more than your culture and the strength of your entire combined team.." Ian gave him a straight, serious look.

Andrew was shocked. If he didn't toughen up, he'd be a 'C-Player' himself.

Not likely. He wasn't about to take the chop from a company he'd grown to care for.

The truth dawned: this was the best bloody job he'd ever had.

COMMENTARY: 'THE A-PLAYER GRID'

As Jim Collins said in his seminal book 'Good to Great' (William Collins, 2001), one of the major challenges in business is all about "getting the right people in the right seats, doing the right things right."

So how do we know whether the people we have are 'the right people'?

I am sure there are other names but I refer to this tool as the 'A Player Grid'. It is a simple 2 x 2 grid which measures the performance of an individual along the X axis and the demonstration of our core values along the Y axis.

Core values	B Player	A Player
	C Player	C Player
	Performance	

For this model to work, we need to be able to measure two things: performance and the practice of our core values.

To ascertain 'performance', every team member should have ideally a single metric against which they are measured. Typically, there'll be a range of numbers against which people are measured; narrowing this down to one number can be a challenge. But if there is no number, how on earth can anyone judge whether someone is doing a good job or not? If there is more than one number what do you do if some numbers are achieved and others are not?

This metric should be very clear. It should form part of the job holder's job description and be spelled out in their current mission status. That way, both the manager and the job holder can clearly assess whether the job holder is performing to a high level or not.

'Core Values' alludes to the job holder's understanding of what the business is about; that their behaviour is in line with the organisation's stated core values. Ideally, the core values should be illustrated with clear examples of the types of behaviour that are 'in line with' or 'out of line with' core values. There should be frequent discussions so that it can be perfectly clear whether a business's core values are being practiced or flaunted by the members, individually or as a group. This makes judgement of low or high adherence to those core values clear and easy.

Someone who can demonstrate high performance and high demonstration of the core values is called an 'A-Player'. The future for them is obvious: onward and upward. They are the exemplary members of our team.

Similarly, those who constantly perform at a low level and don't exemplify our core values are 'C-Players'. For them, too, the decision is easy: we have to exit those individuals. We will never create a great or even a good business with people who neither perform nor behave well. We must release them; hopefully, they can excel somewhere more suited to them.

Those people who demonstrate our core values, who 'get' what we are about, but don't perform at a high enough level - these are the people we need to work on to help to get their performance up to an acceptable level. This may involve a variety of interventions including a change in job, position or location. We don't want to lose them, but we may have to if we can't help them perform at a high enough level. It is only right and proper that they know and understand where they sit in the A player grid and why.

The most challenging of the quadrants is the bottom right hand corner. These people perform well but don't demonstrate our core values. They are labelled 'C-Players', and we must exit them.

Why?

Well, they are the most dangerous people on our team. They are the people who are performing well but who don't behave in a way that aligns with our core values. They are potentially the saboteurs in the camp. This will be the salesman that sells a lot but never sells a second time to the same person; he creates a lot of dissatisfied customers and letters of complaint, while we are trying to build a relationship based and repeat purchase type of business. Every success he has undermines our strategy and actually encourages others to follow suit.

Why would we not try to get them to change their ways?

Of course, that would be great, but experience shows that core values relate to the way we are - not just how we behave during office hours. It is likely that the 'C-Player' won't be able to change sufficiently to be able to align to our core values; keeping him in position is only ever likely to erode and undermine the culture of the business.

It's a great exercise to plot every member of a business's team on the grid and to work out what proportion of the team are 'A-Players'. It is usually quite an eye-opener!

CHAPTER 23

With her head in her hands, Lynne sat at her desk letting the rush slip away from her for a few, deadly slow minutes. She felt as though she were being strangled.

But she'd done it.

The whole presentation had been sent, never to be clawed back again. There was no room for regrets, second thoughts or even blaming anybody else for her actions. This time, it was all down to her.

It was so much more than just a presentation, mind you. She'd delivered and presented hundreds of them before. This time, she knew that everything was on the line. Her job, her company, her family.

If this failed – and how could it not, really? – she would lose her standing with everybody around her, and her relationship with both of her parents. Hell, even Fay. As much as she hated to admit it to herself, Fay mattered, too.

What choice had she had, though?

Something had to be done fast, not just for Erimus Manufacturing's sake, but for her own, too. She knew deep down that just one more half-arsed attempt on her part to look as though she were pulling her weight would be the end of the last shred of self-respect she had. Irrespective of what her father thought, let alone said, about her performance and herself as a person, her own opinion mattered much more.

This was it. Win or lose, she'd met herself head on, really stretched for something seemingly unattainable for the first time in her life. She felt cut loose: bereft, alone, insecure - but curiously free, unstoppable and completely empowered at the same time.

After a couple of minutes when her breath had returned, she looked up and turned her head towards the office area. Through her window, she saw Natalie on the phone, Pete tapping away under his headphones at his computer, Roxy and Andrew leaning against the window sill drinking coffee and laughing together.

For God's sake. Didn't they have anything better to do? She watched them for a moment and suddenly felt tired. Not just in a 'I need a ten-minute break' way; this time, it was a bone-weary, end of herself feeling. She felt completely empty.

She watched Ian as he walked across the office space from the kitchen towards the stairs to the car park, and she was drawn to her door before he disappeared. She opened it and walked into the open plan area, hoping for the normal hubbub and common office sounds of life going on as normal to calm her.

The volume level fell as she stepped into the space, however, and she was left instead with the knowledge that every head in the place had turned to look at her.

Expecting what, exactly? Had any of these idiots any bloody idea what her life was like? What she'd been through over the last two weeks? What she'd just done, for Christ's sake?

She looked back at them bleakly, imagining that none of them would be there this time next month on account of her sending the presentation – and not a single one of them had a clue that the end was coming. The pressure built inside her head, pounding and growing more intense until their faces blurred together. She heard herself somewhere far away, screaming at them.

"For God's sake – I did what I could!"

Her phone left her right hand at the speed of light and smashed on the wall just to the right of Andrew's head as she half ran from the room.

Everything froze.

Andrew looked at his hands to make sure he was alive. Roxy stared at Ian to see what he would do. Ian stared at the door where Lynne had disappeared. The rest of the staff looked at each other – frozen in what they had been doing just before her rant.

Pete was the first one to arrive back in the moment. With a wobbly attempt at a grin, he addressed Ian, standing mute and shocked next to the stairwell.

"Things must be improving. She used to get through at least two phones a month."

Andrew arrived back in the office after a long spell in the workshop later that afternoon. Things were moving well there; many of the team members seemed to be getting along better and working more efficiently than before, and none of them had even met Ian. Two, though, were still not engaging, even though they weren't doing a bad job. Not exactly mavericks, but not entirely on-board yet, either.

Could it be that his own behaviour had changed so much that most of his staff were feeling some of its positive effects?

He was fairly confident that he wasn't imagining it.

Tired but happy, he switched on his pc, settled down in his chair and opened his email. Speak of the devil, he thought, as he clicked on the most recent mail.

From: Ian Kinnery

To: Andrew Willis

Subject: Get a cup of coffee – time for a story!

Hi, Andrew –

Thought I'd share with you a story that an amazing coach told me once. It changed the way I think, and it struck me that it applies to what we were discussing the other day.

Happy reading!

THE FABLE OF JOHNNY AND JIMMY

One winter's morning, Johnny was delighted to find that it had snowed overnight. He tore downstairs, yelling as he went.

"Mum! Mum! It's snowed! Can I go out to play?"

His mum tried to calm him down a bit.

"Johnny, it will be freezing out there. Stay inside with me where it is warm. You can see the snow just as well from in here."

But Johnny was determined. "Mum! Please, please, please can I go and play in the snow?"

He was relentless. Eventually, he wore his mother down.

Then, as the majority of mothers across the world would do, she said, "Oh, alright, Johnny. If you must go and play in the snow you can, but let's get you ready first," and with those words she dressed little Johnny in his wellies, thick socks, warmest clothes, waterproofs, hat, scarf and gloves. As soon as she let him loose, he ran to the back door to play in the snow in the garden.

In the house next door a similar scene was playing out.

As soon as Jimmy looked outside, he hurtled down the stairs shouting, "Mum, Mum! Can I go and play in the snow?"

Now, Jimmy's mum was a little different. She, too, tried of all the usual strategies to dissuade Jimmy from going outside. When she realised it was impossible she looked calmly at her son.

"Now, look here, Jimmy: if you want to go and play outside in the snow, that's fine by me. But before you do, is there anything you should think about?"

Jimmy glimpsed Johnny already outside, busy making a snowman. He was desperate to go and join him.

'No, Mum! I just want to go outside and play in the snow!"

"Are you sure, Jimmy?" She asked again.

'No, Mum! I just want to go outside and play in the snow!"

She paused for just a second.

"Well, if you're absolutely sure … " and she opened the door for him.

Little Jimmy bolted outside, still dressed in his pyjamas and slippers, to play in the snow.

You can imagine what happened next. Jimmy's shrieks of delight at being with his pal outside in the snow soon dried up. He was cold and wet, and within five minutes he was crying and knocking at the door to be let back in.

His mum wasn't a total ogre and had been keeping a watchful eye on Jimmy from the window. She was instantly there with warm towels to dry him, a warm drink to bring his temperature back up and a cuddle by the fire to comfort him.

A little later, bundled up in his dressing gown by the fire, Jimmy's enthusiasm had returned. With all the resilience that kids show he started again.

"Mum! Mum! Can I go and play in the snow?"

His mum took a deep breath and smiled. "Jimmy, of course you can, if that is what you still want to do. But before you do, is there anything that you need to think about?"

This time, Jimmy remembered the pain that the deep, deep cold had caused him and was aware that Johnny had played out for a lot longer than Jimmy had been able to. He considered this before answering his mum.

"Well, Mum, my feet got very wet and cold so perhaps I should wear my wellies."

"Okay," said his mum, practically. "Anything else?"

Jimmy thought a little harder.

"Wellies will keep my feet dry," he mused, "but I'll need socks to keep them warm. I should put on thick socks ..."

Look, I'll resist the temptation to turn this into a real shaggy dog story, but you can imagine the rest of the process. Jimmy eventually went out into the snow having taken his own decisions about his clothing. He was now properly equipped, and he had a great time playing in the snow – building a bigger snowman than Johnny's.

You may ask, "What's he on about, now? What's the moral of this fable?"

Well, fast forward fifteen or twenty years in the story and ask yourself who you'd rather have on your team: Johnny, who had never made a decision for himself in his life, or Jimmy, who'd been encouraged to make thousands of decisions for himself?

More importantly, Jimmy had learned the connections between the decisions he makes and the consequences of those decisions. He'd learned to take ownership, accountability and responsibility for his decisions.

So, Andrew - which one would you pick?

To Your Success,

Ian

Andrew smiled. It was food for thought. Johnny and Jimmy deserved a medal for services to industrial relations.

COMMENTARY: 'THE MEANING OF THE JOHNNY & JIMMY FABLE'

The answer is clear: Jimmy would make a far better employee, team member and leader.

Although our motives may be the best, every time we make a decision for someone we deprive them of the chance to learn for themselves, and in so doing we cheat them of the opportunity to learn and to grow.

Of course, learning cannot happen without mistakes. Getting it wrong is a necessary part of the learning process. The 'learning world' is not a perfect world, without risks or mistakes.

How often, with our family and with our team, do we take the short term, expedient option of telling someone what to do, rather than the slightly longer term but ultimately more beneficial choice of helping them to learn and to grow?

Do we want to grow a business and a generation of Johnnies or Jimmies?

The fable of Johnny and Jimmy is a cornerstone of my coaching philosophy but I cannot take credit for it. It is based upon a story Sir John Whitmore told me a few years ago. As a great coach, he helped bring to light something I was probably always aware of deep down but couldn't really see; in so doing, he helped me make better future choices.

There are several implications that spring from the story.

Firstly, Jimmy's Mum would have to have complete faith that her son was capable of learning the lessons that Life was about to teach him. She had to have faith that he would be able to work out what he could do to not get cold and wet the next time. She would have had to have faith that he was capable of thinking for himself and coming up with the answers that were best for him.

Conversely, we'd have to conclude that Johnny's mum didn't have the same faith in him. She had chosen – perhaps not consciously - to make Johnny's decisions for him. The more she did so, the less likely it became that Johnny made own decisions. The more she persisted, the more she would be leading Johnny to a position of 'learned helplessness'.

Johnny would learn that he didn't have to think for himself because his mum had taught him, by custom and practice, that he didn't need to. His mum would always answer his questions for him. You can imagine an eighteen-year old Johnny saying to his mum, "I'm going to the football this afternoon. What should I wear?"

In the light of this fable, our giving people the answers rather than helping them to find them for themselves now feels disrespectful. It demeans the other person in the relationship ... especially if we assume that other human beings are inherently good, intelligent, imaginative, capable of choice and solving problems.

The fable of Johnny and Jimmy illustrates one thing above all to me: the value of our gift to be able to choose. By making choices for other people we steal not only their gift - their right to choose - but also their greatest opportunity: the opportunity to learn. If we knew that was the price of our actions, would we willingly make that choice?

To quote from Nancy Kline, "The quality of everything human beings do, everything- depends on the quality of the thinking we do first".

To help us to be the best that we can be we must encourage each other to think for ourselves. The greatest gift we can offer each other is the framework in which to do so.

CHAPTER 24

To: Lynne Peston

From: Edgar Watson

Subject: INVITATION TO APPLY

Dear Lynne,

Thank you for sending us your proposal for the STADIA UK DEVELOPMENTS site in Middlesbrough.

We appreciate the amount of work you have done so far in order to compile your ideas on method, execution and costs.

As you are aware, there are several companies applying for this contract, a few of them nationals with a larger infrastructure than that of ERIMUS MANUFACTURING to handle the demanding amount of work and timescale to which we are committed to see the new stadium built.

However, the committee has agreed that your proposal is one that we would like to hear more about. Especially promising was the notion of the work possibly being carried out by a company that has its roots in the region: the real deal for the North East population – built by the North East for the North East. The idea appealed to our marketing team.

On that basis, we would like to invite you to our offices on Monday in two weeks' time at 2.00p.m. to talk with us more about your ideas and projections. Please be aware that there will be two other companies visiting us that day for the same invitation, and yours will be the final presentation.

Please let me know if that time is amenable. We look forward to meeting you and your presentation team.

Yours faithfully,

Edgar Watson

Managing Director, Stadia UK Developments

To: Andrew Willis; Fay Peston

From: Lynne Peston

Hi,

Please set aside half an hour from two 'o clock for an urgent meeting in my office today.

With thanks –

Lynne

CHAPTER 25

Andrew had only twenty minutes left of a lunch hour to get something to eat before he was due in with Lynne and Fay for their hastily-arranged meeting.

What was this about? Had she heard that Fay had found out about Sean in the worst possible way?

He asked Roxy for one of her packets of soup; it would have to do until later. He needed to try and find Fay, who'd left the Tuesday @ 12 meeting forty minutes ago looking like death warmed up. She'd had a genuine shock. Andrew wanted to see if she was alright before he went into the meeting with her.

She was a funny one, that one. While she did all she could to destabilise people with her snide remarks, she'd been with them since they'd started this new process with Ian and had grown, too. Every now and then, she even showed a friendly side.

He wasn't the only one who'd noticed it. Natalie and Roxy had, too, and it showed earlier when Natalie had put her arm around her to comfort her at the news.

She would never have done that two months ago.

He sighed. It would be sad to lose her; surely she wouldn't quit, would she?

He discovered Fay talking softly with Roxy and Natalie in the kitchen. Not the best place, he thought, as the gossip flew around this area like gnats at a fishpond. Still, he wasn't about to break up their girls' conversation, and he noted as he left them that that was another thing that wouldn't have happened before now.

He drank his soup sitting at his desk and waited for Fay to arrive, and together they walked to Lynne's office door.

"You alright?" he asked her under his breath before he knocked.

She nodded, giving him a quick smile. She squared her shoulders as her sister called them inside and walked in calmly, if a little stiffly.

"Great, guys – thanks for coming at short notice," Lynne began with uncharacteristic, upbeat humour. "Close the door – I have some news."

Andrew closed the door behind him. Has she found her prince at last? He hoped so – maybe she just needed a lover.

"I haven't told you about this yet because I wanted to be sure first," she began, and Andrew felt Fay tense beside him. "Basically, the pressure's been on us to come up with a fast way to sort out the big tax bill we were left with last year," she left out any allusion to the branch's being on the line. No need to scare them just yet. "Well – we have a chance to make it up, and a hell of a lot more besides!"

She was like a schoolkid on break-up day, Andrew thought, although his curiosity was piqued.

"I pitched an idea to 'Stadia UK Developments' – you know, the company that holds the contract for the new stadium? They liked it, and – well, they want us to present to them next Monday. It's really happening!"

Andrew was floored; he would never have guessed that this was coming.

Nor would he have guessed what came next. Fay went into meltdown.

"You complete, lying bitch!" she screamed suddenly at her sister. "You think it's okay to sneak around doing things behind people's backs? Who were you aiming this one at, Lynne?"

Everything stopped. Lynne was completely blindsided.

"Wh – what?" she stammered, feeling for the edge of her desk to regain her balance.

Fay kept coming at her.

"You aggressive, two-faced cow! How dare you fire my staff without speaking to me first! You think I'm going to help you out with some new-fangled idea that you reckon will win Dad over? Huh?"

By now she was in Lynne's face; Andrew thought that there might be a fistfight.

Lynne backed away, white with shock. Andrew glanced out of the window and saw to his horror that every single person in the office had stopped what they were doing and was watching, jaw on the floor, hearing every word that was being shouted.

Fortunately, it finished as fast as it began.

"Forget it!" Fay turned on her heel and tore out of the room, stopping only to snatch up her laptop and her bag before running out of the office.

The silence was cut only by two unanswered phones in the open plan area, their owners struck dumb.

"Looks like it's down to you and me, then, Andrew," Lynne staggered back and sank heavily into her chair.

Andrew had no words.

PART 6

"For things to change, you have to change. For things to get better, you must get better."

JIM ROHN, entrepreneur and speaker

IAN KINNERY

To: Ian Kinnery

From: Andrew Willis

Subject: Trouble at the office

Hi, Ian –

Hope you're enjoying your holiday.

Thought I'd better drop you a line and put you in the picture – there's been a slight crisis at the office. Lynne and Fay have finally come to serious blows and Fay's walked out.

I don't know if it's for good. Lynne hasn't said anything to me about it – but I was there when it happened.

She had called Fay and me in to her office to tell us about a massive pitch she's put together and wants us to help her present (maybe she's told you about this already? It's worth millions!). Fay was upset already, though, because she'd just found out in our Tuesday @ 12 meeting that Lynne fired Sean. Apparently, she had no idea.

I decided (as a WWW) that I would speak to her later in the day when she'd calmed down, and see if we could get to the root of why the bad blood between them interferes with our work so often.

That was the plan, but Lynne spoke to us first in her office and Fay just flew off the handle. They were edging for a punch up – it was that bad.

I left them and tried to appease everyone on the floor, but several people on Roxy's team were rattled.

Anyway – thought I'd let you know – give you a bit of warning about what you might walk into next week. Roxy and I are going to see if we can rally the troops a bit in the meantime.

Also, I'm going to be busy helping Lynne with this presentation. I had no idea she was cooking up something this big. Fingers crossed.

See you then – enjoy the ride!

Andrew"

PART 7

"Never doubt that a small group of thoughtful, committed citizens can change the world; indeed, it's the only thing that ever has."

MARGARET MEAD, anthropologist

CHAPTER 26

With Lynne and Fay out of the way, it seemed like the perfect time to get cracking on cleaning up the office and have a bit of fun at the same time.

Andrew and Roxy had taken it on themselves to get the place cleaned up – not just from a safety point of view but for their own sakes, too. Who wanted to work in this junkyard?

Andrew had been systematically reorganising and tidying the workshop area for the last three weeks, and it was almost in the state he'd be proud to show it off to anybody. He had one week left to get it in order so that he could meet the deadline he gave himself in front of the other managers. It was a WWW so they'd hold him accountable to it, he knew.

As he was now committed to attend the major presentation with Lynne, he asked Natalie to stand in for him on the day as his team's leader. She jumped at the chance – loving a bit of goodhearted competition. From that moment, she and Roxy came up with some great ideas for getting everybody motivated and happy on the day.

Roxy had sent an email to her Sales and Hire team a week in advance:

Subject: Special Office Day

"Hi, Everybody –

Make sure that you do not make any appointments or other plans for next Monday. We will be having a Special Office Day, and you need to come in comfy, casual clothes. A chance to dress down! ☺

It'll be lots of fun, and everybody is to attend – but I can't tell you much more about it than that.

Please diarise!

Roxy"

She kept it mysterious so that none of her team could wriggle out of it, of course, but she understood how important it was for them to have fun while they cleaned up and she went to great lengths to prepare a happy day for them.

Using the Sales budget, she bought enough pairs of rubber gloves, disposable aprons, silly mob caps and detergents to tackle any kind of yuck in existence (and there was bound to be a lot – the place probably hadn't been cleaned in years). Buckets, mops, sponges, cloths – the works. She invested the rest in cakes and snacks – only to be brought out of the kitchen when the bulk of the work had been done – and set some aside to treat everyone at lunchtime to a large order of pizza to be delivered by the local Italian favourites.

Lynne was going to be out all day with Andrew, and of course, Fay was off. Nobody was going to dampen the team's spirits for The Great Black Bag Day.

Together, she and Natalie drew up a list of all the things that needed to be done and a rough timeline in which to complete the whole job. When Andrew heard about the plans, he decided that, as his own team's challenge, he'd have them complete the tidying efforts on the workshop floor on the same day. It would be fun to have the two teams competing together; what a great way to get them mingling and interacting!

When Monday came, the whole staff turned up curious to see what awaited them. Roxy and Natalie were already there to explain, and they held a combined meeting in the open plan area of the office, with Andrew's team feeling a little out of place and teasing the sales execs.

They loved the idea of having a change of routine.

"So, the race is on, everybody," said Roxy, energising them all with her infectious sense of fun. "Pete will be the overall judge who decides which team has done a better job at the close of the day …"

"The other team's been cleaning up forever already!" laughed one of her team.

"Yes, but they have at least five times the area and a jungle of equipment; where they are right now is a fair comparison, we feel. So stop your moaning," Roxy teased, and Andrew's team cheered her.

Pete, who'd just arrived, was astonished to find so many people in the office. He stopped in his tracks and listened to Roxy speak, amazed at how she held their attention and entertained them – really worked them up. He stood at the back smiling until Roxy picked on him to be the final judge, and bowed graciously as everyone turned to look at him. This could be fun, he thought, and tried to imagine what it would look like in there, clean and fresh for once.

"So, is everybody ready for 'The Great Black Bag Challenge'?" Roxy provoked them tirelessly.

Everybody yelled, and Natalie threw out the packets of rubber gloves and aprons to them all. They grabbed and scrambled for them, thoroughly enjoying themselves already. At Roxy's 'Go!' they beetled about, Andrew's team heading downstairs with Natalie as their leader for the day, and Roxy's team donning their gear.

To incentivise her team once the others had left the office area, Roxy took a ten pound note and, just for fun, climbed onto a desk and stuck it on the ceiling.

"There," she announced, "that's an extra perk for the first one to get your own desk area tidy – and that means vacuuming your area, too!"

They all cheered and dived into the process. Pete looked about him as he settled down at his own desk. Who knew anyone could get so excited about cleaning? He was impressed with Roxy – great job!

For the next two hours, there was a frenzy of organising. Fourteen big black refuse bags full of outdated paperwork that needed recycling, an endless stream of cups, spoons and plates going to the kitchen to be washed and put away, personal bits and bobs on everybody's desk that was either thrown out or dusted off and kept. Landline phones, pc monitors and keyboards were all disinfected and shined, the windows were washed and even the sickly fern was replaced with a new, flowering shrub that Roxy had bought at the weekend.

The same whirlwind was happening downstairs, with lots of scrubbing of walls, shelves and the floor. Everybody flung themselves at the task, and Natalie was amazed to see how fast things improved. It seemed to do so much for everybody's mood. Spirits were high, and so would Andrew's be when he came back and saw the improvement.

At the thought of Andrew, she felt a twinge of apprehension for him. What was going on in their presentation?

CHAPTER 27

Andrew gripped his seatbelt and wished he'd bought train tickets instead. He wasn't a good passenger at the best of times and Lynne was driving like a bat out of hell southwards on the M1 in full rush hour traffic.

As other drivers flashed their lights in warning and moved hurriedly out of her way, she prattled on about the upcoming presentation: who was to say what, at exactly which point, what to avoid saying, how to look, pose, move – everything they'd rehearsed a dozen times already.

He nodded apologetically to the woman in the car next to them as they overtook her and she mouthed something unfriendly at them. Little point in going over all this stuff again if we don't even make it to London in one piece, he thought.

Their presentation was booked for 2:00 pm and for some reason Lynne had insisted on driving.

"I don't trust the train. What if there's a delay?"

For two weeks, she and Andrew had worked at every opportunity to plan, write and rehearse a routine that was now pitch-perfect. She was to take the main points of the presentation, as representative of Erimus Manufacturing, and Andrew was to present a short video they'd had made on the way they worked and the skills they had, examples of some of their bigger constructions and a few testimonials from worthy-sounding clients. Questions and answers would be handled between the two of them, with Lynne deciding in each case who should answer.

"We must appear as slick as possible," she stated unnecessarily, and Andrew bit his lip to keep himself from a snippy retort.

When she'd arrived at his house at 6:30 am on the morning of the presentation, she'd woken up the entire street with a blast on the horn and a yell through the open passenger door to "Andrew – move your arse!", only to send him back inside again to change his tie.

He needn't have worried. They arrived at Stadia UK Developments at least an hour early and settled to wait in the large, impressive reception.

Awards adorned the walls, with photographs of prestigious presentations and businesspeople clasping hands with various executives of the company. There were two receptionists behind a well-lit, sleek front desk with the tallest vase of lilies Andrew had ever seen. Everything about the place was designed to impress the visitor and intimidate rivals.

His stomach rumbled and he checked his watch. There'd be time to go for a sandwich, but Lynne swore that she couldn't face the thought of food. He didn't trust her in the reception on her own: you just never knew who might walk in and be dragged into her nervous chatter. He satisfied himself with a cup of coffee and tried to ignore all of Lynne's last-minute stage notes.

At 1:30 pm, three smart young businessmen emerged from a corridor, smiling and chattering excitedly as they headed for the reception desk. As they signed themselves out, Andrew distinctly heard them refer to the stadium construction site and Lynne grabbed his sleeve manically, going puce in the face and blinking in panic.

"The competition!" she hissed, and he didn't have the heart to remind her that they were but a small part of it.

He just smiled at her reassuringly and prayed that she'd hold it together for the presentation. He'd never seen her so jumpy. A little stage fright was always good for a presentation, but too much could ruin it. As for himself, he felt nervous too, but as she was carrying most of the can he was looking forward to observing how the big businesses did it.

What was the expression? 'If you want to play with the big dogs you've got to learn to pee in the tall grass.'

One day, he grinned to himself, he'd make that a sign and put it up in the reception at Erimus Manufacturing.

A long, agonising half an hour later, one of the receptionists broke the silence.

"Lynne Peston and Andrew Willis?"

Lynne jolted upright, knocking the glass coffee table in front of them with her knee as Andrew nodded in response and stood.

"You can go in now, please," she said. "Straight down the corridor, second door on the right."

Lynne wiggled her suit straight as she trotted ahead of Andrew, glancing back it him just once with a worried grimace and exaggeratedly waving crossed fingers in his face. She knocked on the door, waited for the response and they burst into a sunny, bright boardroom with the biggest table Andrew had ever seen.

He had to blink a couple of times to acclimatise to the sunlight as it streamed in through a window that looked over a breathtaking view of Victoria Embankment and the Thames. He smiled at the five executives who sat on the far side of the table welcoming them in.

"Welcome, both of you," said one of them, as he introduced himself as Edgar Watson and the rest of his team.

It's going to be alright, breathed Andrew, as he and Lynne shook hands with them all and settled their briefcases onto two chairs positioned for them at the table.

The room was a minimalist work of art, with every gleaming gadget and piece of equipment necessary for a top performance. The walls bore two large Picasso prints on a sunny shade of peach, which helped to soften the edge of intimidation in the air. The five hosts were friendly enough, save one of the two women who managed a quick flick of a smile before staring at them both piercingly for the rest of the meeting.

While Lynne gushed her introduction, Andrew quietly connected his laptop to the HDML line ready for them. He breathed a sigh of relief when the large screen to his right lit up the opening frame of his video, pausing obediently until his turn came to speak.

They were given fifteen minutes to present, with an extra fifteen to take questions afterwards. They had timed it religiously in their preparations, and had rehearsed their responses to what they thought would be the most likely questions asked, and as far as Lynne knew they had accounted for every minute down to the last second.

As far as Lynne knew.

As he listened to her stumbling slightly and getting flustered in her first three minutes of talking, Andrew dug his nails into the palms of his hands and wondered how she'd react to the little changes he'd made to his part of the presentation the night before.

"So without further ado," she laughed nervously, four minutes and twenty-five seconds in, "I shall hand over to my colleague, Andrew Willis, who's going to give you a visual insight into who we are and how we are able to bring this dream to life. Afterwards, I'll discuss figures and plans."

She nodded at Andrew, gulping in relief that her first part was over, and flopped heavily into her chair, reaching with shaking hands for the glass of water in front of her.

Andrew stood up and tried to swallow the lump that had suddenly lodged itself in his throat. He didn't know what he was more scared of: the five pairs of eyes that were fixed on him from over the table or Lynne's eruption later when she'd found out what he'd done.

It wasn't much, really. Just a few extra slides that he'd added to play after the video's ending that he felt added an extra angle to the narrative that had occurred to him too late to discuss with Lynne. He knew she'd be livid, but he really believed that they were significant.

He closed the huge blinds and pressed 'enter' on his laptop, taking a deep breath and folding his arms.

"Welcome to Erimus Manufacturing ..." the male voice over began over the uplifting music bed, and eight minutes of scenes from the workshop floor, the newly cleaned office, happy staff faces, brief comments from the confident management team and three client testimonials absorbed everyone in the room.

As the music ended and the visual on screen faded, Andrew moved forward and started to speak as Lynne began to stand up for her next section.

"Now that you've met our team," he began, "I'd like to introduce you to another character. One that you've met before, but cannot know as well as we do."

He clicked 'enter' on his laptop once more, ignoring Lynne's frozen look of horror as she half-stood in the dim light, and the screen lit up with a panoramic view of a beautiful, North East landscape, the words "ERIMUS: WE SHALL BE" slowly appearing in the foreground.

There hadn't been time to record a voice over for this part, so Andrew settled into talking over each slide for an impromptu four minutes.

He spoke with pride and confidence about the history of the area, how since early times the people of the North East had been experts in manufacturing; how the area was enriched with ore and assets that the rest of the country had envied and relied upon for centuries, how the land had borne generations of people with heart and strength and how the Industrial Revolution had seen the North East become the bedrock for the largest Empire the world had ever known. As he spoke, historic pictures of the area's development brought his narrative to life.

"It was a struggle," he said with emotion, "a fight for survival and a dream that our people took on for the rest of the nation, and we called Middlesbrough 'Erimus', meaning 'we shall be'. We shall be strong, we shall be counted, we shall thrive – not just as a community, but as a vital part of the nation. Nobody understands the character of the North East as we do …" he paused as he flicked to the last slide – a picture of the whole team together taken on the proposed site itself that Roxy had persuaded them to pose for one weekend. "You can have confidence in us as a team, as we work together in an open, honest, empathic way which, as you can see, delivers more than our clients' expectations. We're passionate about this project, because we are Erimus Manufacturing. We belong here, and together with you, 'We shall be'."

There was a long pause.

He made his way to undraw the blinds as everybody, including Lynne, digested what they'd just learned.

How the hell did he know all that stuff? She wanted to smack him, but she was overawed and, luckily for him, glued to her seat.

She watched in amazement as the executives spontaneously applauded him – all except old Vinegar Tits at the end of the row who merely wrote notes in her file without looking up. That'll show you, she thought smugly, and for a moment forgot entirely to be mad at Andrew.

He thanked them, handed over to Lynne, and took his place with trembling knees. She took over with more confidence, fielded virtually all of the questions and even cracked a joke with Edgar.

If he was lucky, and she didn't finish them both off with her driving on the way home, he might just survive today after all.

CHAPTER 28

Andrew pulled at his short sideburns as he stared at his computer screen.

It was 11:45 am and the 'Tuesday @ 12' meeting was looming. Perhaps it was best that it was finally happening. It had been taking so long to get here, and looking about him, the others were dreading it, too.

Over the desk divide in front of him, Roxy was restless, looking busy as she rifled through papers on her desk but not doing anything with any of them. She looked up once and they exchanged quick, terse smiles. The clock on the wall seemed to have been getting progressively louder all morning as it ticked the seconds away. The countdown had begun. The countdown to what? They were now used to the rhythm of their meeting every Tuesday at 12 but this threatened to be different. This would be the meeting that Lynne would be attending once again. The first since Ian had begun what now seemed to be a quiet revolution.

Ian was already upstairs in the boardroom, gazing around happily and wondering what kind of magician had visited Erimus Manufacturing's Head Office while he'd been gone. The transformation was as sudden as it was complete; he was rarely astounded, but this morning was a sensory overload for even him.

The room itself seemed to pull him in.

"Come on in, lovely friend," it seemed to say, "Relax, be yourself, you're on top form and we want you here …"

The colours embraced him, the sunlight adding an almost romantic lilt to the straight lines and muted formality that clothed the furniture. There was even a new, oak panelled clock on the wall, ticking away sombrely, with a sense of timelessness and enduring comfort, businesslike, functional and yet welcoming.

He'd come in to the office with an extra spring in his step and a beaming smile as he saw the change in the office.

What a transformation! The whole place looked so much brighter, with the sun now able to stream in through sparkling windows, the aisles between the desks clear and even the carpet looked fresher. It couldn't be a new one, could it? He could hardly believe his eyes.

In the kitchen, he'd noticed the old boardroom clock on the wall, with a distinctive mark made in black permanent ink on the number ten.

"So that whenever it gets to ten to twelve on Tuesday, that's when we have to get out of here and into the boardroom," explained Natalie, laughing.

She'd enjoyed taking part in the transformation in her own way – flicking a neck scarf to dust off a plant leaf or two, that sort of thing. She wasn't as hands on as Roxy, or as earthy in taste, but she had an eye for fashion and home décor. She was surprised to find how much she enjoyed looking at the office with a perspective that encouraged a little flair. Individuality, even.

Ian laughed with her and genuinely marvelled at the change he saw all around him. The atmosphere was different, he could sense that now. The team had pride, which in turn fed their passion for their work. If nothing else, he knew that he could leave satisfied on that score. If they could bring their individual skills to the table and work together – well, they'd find the very place where passion and skill meet. The Nirvana of a team that has places to go.

When he was told that the big clean up had been Roxy's and Natalie's undertaking, he was impressed and told them so. They both smiled modestly and said it was nothing – the team had done most of it. He suspected that it had taken a huge amount of energy and planning to accomplish, though, and noted their muted response.

Now, he stood in the transformed boardroom and allowed himself to hope that this room, finally, was where the management team's skill and rediscovered passion would be allowed to flourish. This was a sign that they were ready, if they were willing to work together, to take the business to even higher levels. Without that willingness, they may not clear the very next hurdle.

The prospect of today's meeting was already making their heads spin. It would be a challenge to see whether they could preserve the healthier communication they had developed over recent weeks.

No wonder: it was the first one that Lynne would attend since Ian had started conducting them with the management team. How would Lynne behave? How would she influence the team spirit? Would she add to or detract from their progress?

Ian asked Andrew to show him the workshop floor with its new look. To both distract and relax him. He led Ian downstairs without saying very much, kitted him out with all the safety gear at the door and ushered him in willingly, but with the air of an overworked carthorse heading for the abattoir.

Inside, everybody was busy. They looked up and called out their hellos to the two men, and Ian answered back. Andrew raised his hand in a half wave and mustered up a thin smile.

That whole area was a feast for the eyes. No more Health and Safety issues down here, thought Ian with satisfaction. Everything was in its place. Racked, stacked and labelled. Walkways painted, floors swept; the place even smelled clean. Andrew told him that he'd already had their insurance brokers visit the premises to go over it in detail, and the feedback they'd given him was very positive. The better appearance had even seemed to create a sense of ownership and even pride in the team who worked there.

Still, even his being able to give Ian that piece of news couldn't seem to make him happier.

"Andrew, relax. Nothing is going to happen at the meeting today that we can't handle. Lynne isn't familiar with the new way the team has been conducting the meetings, that's all. Let's take this one step at a time." He looked directly into Andrew's eyes and thought he saw a flicker of hope.

"Stay in the moment, remember."

Andrew fought hard to 'stay in the moment' all morning, but as he mounted the stairs to the boardroom at ten to twelve the feeling of apprehension returned.

Well, he reasoned, at least there couldn't be another bust up between the two sisters this time; Fay still hadn't returned to work. Perhaps that was one of the things that Lynne was going to address in this meeting.

He wondered what Ian would make of it all if Lynne reverted to type.

Everybody save Lynne was in place just before twelve. Natalie had her LB/NT forms with her as well as the WWW ones. She wasn't sure how this was going to turn out, but maybe they'd all get lucky and stay on course with the new way of doing things. Personally, she was glad Ian was still with them and she knew he would take control if things broke down.

Everybody was quiet as they waited for Lynne to join them. Pete had set up his laptop, the month's figures up to date and at the ready to shine on the screen when the right moment arrived. He'd learned from Paul not to show them earlier than that in the meeting as it distracted everyone from the agenda while other important matters were being discussed.

Lynne walked into the boardroom at five past, surprised to see everyone sitting in a neat room, all ready with paper and pens in front of them.

"Hi, everyone," she said, unsmiling.

They all muttered their greetings and waited.

She put her books and mug of tea on the table in front of her and sat down.

"Welcome back, to our weekly management meeting, Lynne," he said, and she smiled in an almost friendly way. "We call it the Tuesday at 12 meeting. And I can see that I should have briefed you better. One of our rules is that the meeting starts promptly at 12, out of respect for each other's time. We would appreciate it if you would treat it with the same respect in future."

You could cut the atmosphere with a knife, Ian thought. He'd chosen to step right into the danger and call out Lynne's behaviour, as he would have done anyone else's. Lynne muttered a shocked "sorry" and before she could utter any excuse Ian moved on.

"Should we start the meeting as we usually do with a follow up of last week's WWW?" He pitched this question at the room in general, although it was intended to be rhetorical.

Natalie blushed. Because of the way the last meeting had ended with Fay's being so upset, she couldn't very well say that the WWW had been for Andrew to talk her down off the ledges. Later,

Fay and Lynne had ended up yelling at each other before he managed to speak to her, and now one of their crew was missing. For the umpteenth time, she felt a sharp pang of pity for Fay.

"The what?" Lynne looked at Ian with a patronising expression from behind her glasses.

"The 'Who, What, When'. It's a part of the process we've developed to drive progress and most of all accountability. At each meeting every decision is recorded on the sheet that Natalie has in front of her right now. We decide 'what' is to be done, by 'whom' and by 'when'. Then, the following week, we are all answerable to each other for the actions we have committed to. That way, things get done. There is no hiding place and we keep each other accountable"

That sounded super-complicated for Lynne's liking. She had to prepare for another meeting later. Let's just move this baby along, she thought.

"That's nice. Well, send each other an email afterwards or something – I have something very important to discuss once I've seen the figures." She suddenly noticed the screen.

"What's all this?" She looked around and Pete shifted uncomfortably. He was used to Lynne's ways, but he'd never known anyone more able to drain the enthusiasm from a room.

Ian insisted that they finished the first item on the agenda; the 'Who What When'. fortunately, every single item from last week had been completed in full and on time. Ian turned the sheet to the team and pointed out the row of green ticks that he had marked against the seven items.

"Well done, team," he said. "All complete, in full and on time. Remember green ticks mean that we are getting traction. Red crosses would mean that we have just been spinning our wheels. Great progress!"

In spite of herself, Lynne was impressed. This was definitely an improvement on previous meetings, after which nothing much seemed to happen.

"Let's look at the numbers, now," Ian announced.

Pete nervously cleared his throat. "I have them here for you," he mumbled, and Andrew felt for him. Poor blighter.

The screen suddenly lit up with the figures as he'd compiled them, the columns clear and accurate, awaiting today's update. Again, Lynne was impressed. This had to be better than the usual, messy scribblings that had previously been part of her weekly meetings. When she saw the figures, though, she changed her mind.

"Right, let's start, then," she said, suddenly and impatiently taking over the meeting. "Andrew."

Each one of them in turn read out their figures for the week, recapping on where they'd been at the end of the previous one. Then, each of them dutifully gave their forecast, with Roxy's voice cracking only a tiny bit when she read out hers.

Why hadn't Lynne familiarised herself with the figures beforehand? They were a matter of record. Lynne was always copied in on the email that confirmed the results of the meeting each week. Ian scribbled a note in his file and waited with the others for her to finish writing everything down.

"Well, you're all a hell of a long way off target for this month, aren't you?" she suddenly snapped. "This is really serious. We're on the same side, guys – and I'm the one who gets it in the neck on your account every week from the Directors. They're visiting us again in a few weeks' time – just after the Regional Awards Night – and if we don't start performing now then there'll be trouble. You've got to remember ..."

Ah, here it comes, Andrew said to himself.

"Nobody is indispensable!" She took of her glasses and pointed straight at each one of them in turn, raising her voice and getting angrier by the second.

"You need to do better, you need to do better and you need to do better! There's no excuse for it. You all know what you're supposed to do. Roxy, I'm disgusted at Sales' performance. If you can't get your team to get the results I want to hear then get rid of the execs you've got and recruit half-decent ones."

Ian glanced over at Roxy who was looking down, writing in her diary with her pen shaking.

"People get lazy when they join Erimus Manufacturing because we're the most established regional company in this industry," she fumed. "They come here and think they've got an easy ride from now on. We're victims of our own success! Well, I tell you, that stops right now."

She paused to let them feel how angry she was. This team was hopeless. Ian hadn't got anywhere with them.

"Right, let's move on."

Ian sat still, feeling the mood in the room deflate like a balloon. He felt for everyone, but kept calm. He needed to think – what was the best plan?

He needed to rebuild some confidence and some goodwill with the team whose worst expectations were being realised in front of their eyes. He couldn't let the meeting end like this. It would take forever to build them back up.

"Okay," he said, "LB and NT"

"What?" barked Lynne.

"LB and NT", Ian calmly replied. "This is when we review and record the successes we have had in the previous week, across the business as a whole"

Lynne snorted and Ian pointed out that she had been receiving copies of the flipchart every week for several weeks. He silently surmised that she hadn't even bothered opening the images.

Given what had gone before, this part of the meeting was slow to gather any momentum. Gradually, one by one, the team started to verbalise their achievements.

Andrew pointed out that, subject to final confirmation, they had ended the previous month with a record-breaking result of £300,000 in sales. Pete jumped on the bandwagon, confirming to a small cheer that his 'flash forecast' would indicate this to be the case.

Someone mentioned a second order from a client that seemed to have left them just two months ago. Ian asked if he could suggest they noted the 'new look' workshop. Roxy followed that up by repeating the feedback from their insurance brokers.

It felt as though the team was using its LB's to wash away the negative effect that Lynne had had on the meeting so far. Happily, it seemed to be working. When Andrew announced that one of the highlights of his week had been in delivering the proposal to Stadia in London with Lynne, the mood in the room rose tangibly.

Lynne leaped into the conversation.

"That was the news I wanted to share with you all earlier," she announced. "Andrew came up with some amazing material right at the last minute – and it totally blew them away!" In truth, she hadn't appreciated his improvisation at the time, but she could see the impression Andrew had made.

Her positivity had little effect on her now despondent team, though. Nobody seemed to be listening to her.

Ian moved on to 'NT' after they had filled a sheet and a half of 'LBs'.

"We didn't start on time today," he commented, noting it on the righthand side of the flipchart. Lynne shifted awkwardly in her seat. The others looked up but avoided making eye contact with Ian in case they laughed or smirked - neither of which would have been an appropriate reaction.

Just before they finished, Ian summed up the meeting.

"Look team, that was a good meeting. It looks like it has been a good week and you're definitely moving yourselves and the business forward. You don't need me to tell you that the month end forecast is disappointing, but it is the first week of the month, after all. Last month, you achieved an all-time record for this business. Not only that, but you improved on your forecast each week, too. You all know what needs to be done to get the performance up to your usual levels. Go to it, and let's see what you can really do."

He could see the looks on their faces. They knew that the best way to get Lynne off their backs was to show her what they were capable of. As long as they could sustain their energy and enthusiasm, Ian knew they would deliver.

Lynne was the first out of the boardroom, having barked her final instructions to the managers about what she wanted each of them to achieve before next Tuesday. She might have to move the meeting - she'd send them an email to confirm.

Everyone was shell-shocked. One by one, the tattered little group rose and edged towards the door without speaking. As he held the door open for Roxy, Ian was surprised to hear her say in a low voice:

"Don't worry. We know better. Maybe we should try the honey method, huh?" and shot him a quick smile.

Honey. Yes. And on thing was for sure: Lynne was due to have a meeting with him, alone, as soon as possible.

From: Lynne Peston

IAN KINNERY

To: Fay Peston

Subject: Please!

Come on, Fay. Please answer my messages. I really want to see you – work this thing out. Happy to meet you away from the office – your choice, I'll get lunch.

Lynne x

CHAPTER 29

Lynne was sitting in Ian's office, pen at the ready and her file paper in front of her, ready to write down Ian's findings from the past two months. Whatever the matter was with the team, she hoped he had some answers by this time.

He was talking about the new way of conducting the meetings that they'd adopted.

"We've been using the 'Who, What, When' system as a way of building a greater culture of accountability and ownership. It seems to be working. They have an ownership and a momentum now. Before we started, did you ever feel as though you were having to push them along, rather than have them pull each other along?"

"Oh, completely. Tell me about it," said Lynne. "It's been like flogging a dead horse at times."

Ian didn't take the bait. Instead, he used the opportunity to follow Lynne's own interest, seeing as it had just presented itself.

"Think of Fury. When you ask him to do something for you and he does it right, you praise him." She nodded. "And if he doesn't do it? Do you punish him?"

"No – if he's learning a new lesson, I just keep praising him for the times he does it right. He gives me more that way, otherwise he'll just be frightened of me and not perform properly at all."

"What do you think would happen if you applied the same technique to your team?"

Lynne pictured herself with the managers in a meeting situation – this time without Ian present. It's true that she hadn't had the benefit of seeing for herself how things had evolved very much over the last several weeks, or the healthier meeting habits of the team as they'd developed. She'd attended just the one meeting, and pehaps hadn't behaved as well as she could have done. She felt uncomfortable about that. Still, she knew that something was very different: she wasn't working with a set of people hellbent on frustrating her and letting her down after all, as she'd always feared. Could she possibly use better techniques with them herself and see better results?

"I don't know ..." she said, so wrapped up in the vision that she forgot for a second that Ian was there with her. "It's not how Dad showed me do things. He's always saying I'm too soft on them and that's why they don't respect me. What if it gets even worse?"

Ian waited for her to refocus on her present, and without a trace of irony asked the big question:

"Lynne, how much worse are you prepared to let it get before you change your actions?"

She looked at him and felt very small. She'd been fighting her fear for so long – fear that she might be responsible for driving the company into the ground after its having been around for so many generations. She'd never live it down, and her father would never forgive her.

Ian had known for some time that this was probably the case.

"You can start small," he said. "You don't have to change everything overnight, and what's more, you don't have to change everything by yourself. That's what your team is there to help you to do. That's the point of having managers. If you look after them, they'll look after their departments. You can see that happening now, while you have been absent from the management meetings," he smiled, trying to lift her spirits a little.

"The way you have been trying to run the business is based on a set of principles that has been handed down from generation to generation and is very outdated, Lynne," he went on, carefully reading her expression. "In some ways, it's unfortunate that you have taken over at a time when none of those old military 'command and control' ways apply in the workplace anymore, and it means that it's fallen to you to change them."

Lynne looked up, interested. This was a perspective she hadn't thought of before.

"You're failing to get the best from your team because they are afraid of you. They are afraid of the style of 'control and command' that you've adopted with them. It is probably a style that you have copied from your father. It may have worked back in the last century. I sense that your own style, your innate and natural style is far removed from that."

She looked blank.

"I have seen you, don't forget."

She looked even more blank.

"I am talking about the empathy you have with your horse." said Ian, spelling it out. She really was blinded by her own fear. "That's your natural style. You know it works with Fury. You should try using it with your team; I expect that you'll start seeing the sort of results that will make you feel proud almost as soon as you do."

"'With every pair of hands comes a free brain'," she quoted him from her first meeting here with him. So, something had struck a chord with her, he thought

He left her to think for a minute as he walked next door to make more coffee. He deliberately took his time, allowing this revelation to settle with her. If she could just take it on board, give it a chance and stand up to the spectre of her fearsome father, she might have a chance. He silently prayed that she would.

Alone with her thoughts for a few minutes, Lynne stared out of the big window, seeing nothing. This was a brand new concept. And besides, it was much sweeter to think about than the terrible mess she was in right now, not just with the company but with her family, too.

What would the managers think of her if she started to use a different management style with them? Would they really think more of her? Get on better?

Actually, she'd noticed that since Ian had been developing them as a team that they were already getting on better. A lot better, in fact.

She picked up her bag and dug around for her phone to see if Fay had been in touch yet. Her fingers closed on a folded sheet of paper and she pulled it out, flattening it on the table in front of her and reading.

PROFESSIONALISM

RESPECT

EXCELLENCE

DUTY

She recognised them at once. Erimus Manufacturing's core values. She'd found them in one of her father's old files that was still in her office. Looking at them now, she wasn't surprised they'd been so hard to remember. They didn't seem to resonate, nor did they seem entirely appropriate now.

Ian walked it with two cups of coffee.

"I found our core values – you asked me for them last time I was here," she said, missing his smile.

"Ah! Go on, then – what are they?"

She read them out and he wrote them in bold letters on the lefthand side of his whiteboard.

"What do you think of those?" he asked, keeping his voice neutral.

"I think we should start enforcing them," she saw his eyebrows raise, "or something," she added.

As he had with Andrew, Ian carefully explained the true nature of core values, what their purpose was and why 'enforcing' them would do nogood whatsoever.

She looked at him with interest. "Do you mean, then, that these core values are wrong for the company?"

"It isn't a case of being right or wrong. Whatever is written on that piece of paper, the Core Values will be whatever the current culture holds to be important. I sense that the company might have outgrown what you have there in the same way as it has the old 'command and control' style of leadership."

They looked at the whiteboard in silence together.

Slowly, deep down inside, Lynne started to feel a sense of growing excitement. They could redefine the core values, couldn't they? To reflect the team as it is today, rather than long ago. 'Professionalism, respect, excellence and duty' might not be entirely bad in their own right, but it did smack of life in the trenches, somewhat.

She suddenly sprang up, taking Ian off guard, and moved quickly to the whiteboard, picking up a different colour pen to the one he'd used. On the righthand side of the board, alongside each of the core values, she started to write.

Next to 'Excellence', she wrote 'Care'. Ian smiled.

"I suppose we'd better keep 'Professionalism'," she said, turning to him for feedback.

"Why? If you all care about each other and your clients, you'll automatically be professional. Keep them simple."

She liked that. "Okay, then. So maybe we could take 'Respect' up a level. The only way I can win Fury's respect is when I show him empathy. I know that. So how about ..." and she wrote 'Empathy' on the board, alongside 'Respect'.

Ian was thrilled. She was making a huge step forwards in front of his very eyes.

"That's great. I like that. Does it feel right to you? Does it reflect the company as you know it?"

It did, and she was already tackling 'Duty'. It didn't matter if they all changed again in the near future; what mattered was that the change was happening, and she was completely motivated, happily thinking not just for herself but for her whole team.

'Duty' was proving a bit trickier. It certainly wasn't right for the team now, but she couldn't think of what should replace it so that the team's sense of duty would simply be a by-product of the way they behaved. Everybody and everything was changing so much that she wasn't sure that she could put her finger on the core value that was already there, intrinsic in the team that was manifesting and evolving at Erimus Manufacturing.

"Tell you what," Ian ventured a suggestion. "Why not put it to the management team? Perhaps they can help come up with that one. The words that you have come up with work for you right now, but remember this is a team game. Why not work on them with the team? I can show you how to go about that. You can always tweak them until the whole group is happy that they fully reflect the reality of who you are and what you collectively consider to be important"

Lynne loved the idea and scribbled everything down in her diary. She only wished that Fay could be a part of it all. She needed her sister, not just as Head of the Middlesbrough branch but also because it just didn't feel right without her. Blood is thicker than water after all.

She discussed it with Ian.

"When you have defined your core values, do you think that Fay would represent them fully? Is she likely to hire people who embody them and commit authentically to talking about them often? The thing is, there has to be a constant demonstration of them, which is why it's so important that everyone intrinsically has them as part of their make-up. Does Fay?"

So far, Lynne could only consider 'Care' and 'Empathy'. Did Fay have those as part of her make up? It might be hard to see, but she'd known her all her life and knew that deep down, she could care very passionately indeed. She didn't trust Fay on the 'empathy' one, though. She was constantly sabotaging Lynne with passive-aggressive jibes and suspected that she might be even worse with some of the other leadership team.

"I think 'Trust' might be a strong possibility," she scribbled down before answering Ian. "I don't really trust her. She flew off the handle in front of the team the other day because of something she perceived I'd done personally to her."

Ian didn't let on that he already knew about the Sean debacle.

"There are three tests for core values: firstly, they have to be alive and authentic in the business today - practiced all the time, talked about and demonstrated. Not just a few words on a bit of paper. Secondly, you need to be brave enough to take a financial hit to preserve them. And thirdly, you need to be brave enough to fire an offender. If Fay cannot reflect or commit to the core values that you will decide on soon, she can never be an A player. She can never be a worthy member of the leadership team and therefore she needs to go."

Lynne blinked. Fire Fay?

Ian waited.

"But she's my sister. I'm not sure I could do that – the whole family would go raving mad."

Ah. Now we've reached the crux of the matter, Ian thought. It was time to pose the central question that affected the choices she made regarding her management style, and thus her actions, too. This was the moment that she would come face to face with her dilemma and make a conscious choice of which path to follow.

Whichever it would be, it would affect the whole future of Erimus Manufacturing.

He shifted slightly, and levelled with her.

"You know, Lynne, there is a fundamental question that I ask all owners of family businesses: is the purpose of the business to serve the family, or is the purpose of the family to serve the business - including its people, its customers and its shareholders? Which is it for you?"

Lynne stared at him, unseeing. The question reached into her mind, going deeper with each passing second and splintering into so many more. It was a truly dizzying moment of revelation; she followed its path into her deepest consciousness, lighting up her reason as it travelled.

Her father would say that the business is there to serve the family. That is the way it had always been. He'd inherited it from his father, and back then the business provided employment for many of the local families. They had a vested interest in it, as did the Pestons.

But what of now? There was no relationship between the staff and the family. The community focus of yesteryear was long gone. Little wonder, then, that the staff members weren't engaged. If the family didn't care about them, why should they care about the family?

After a long pause, she looked at Ian, quite exhausted from all of this rapid, deep thinking.

"We need to serve the business," she said simply. She imagined herself telling her father this, and felt suddenly strong, full of conviction.

Ian grabbed his opportunity.

"Then you and Fay both need to stop bringing family issues into your professional lives and working relationship with each other. Perhaps your task is to resolve to put your father's influence firmly to one side and work with the great opportunity you've been given. Fay has a responsibility, as a member of the leadership team, to all of the stakeholders and must start behaving professionally, without bringing her petty sister-spats into the office. If she can't do that ..."

Lynne nodded, straight-faced.

She's got it, he thought.

One day, he'd have to write a book about all this.

COMMENTARY: 'INSPIRE BY LOVE OR RULE BY FEAR'

One of the greatest changes in modern times can be seen in the psychology and make-up of the business leaders of the greater part of the western world.

In 1960, Douglas McGregor identified two different ways of managing which he called 'Theory X' and 'Theory Y'. 'Theory X' represented the assumptions of traditional management, authoritarian 'command and control', whereas 'Theory Y' held that people were inherently motivated by curiosity and the pleasure they could derive from their using their own skills and creativity.

When he wrote "The Human Side of Enterprise" (McGraw-Hill, 1960), McGregor wanted people to challenge their assumptions. Many modern managers find themselves caught in a dilemma between these two management styles. Should they be authoritarian or motivational? The truth is that neither style is right nor wrong. Come to that, neither is easy to do well.

Hence the dilemma.

As one of my own coaches says, "There is no right or wrong; there are only choices." Our choosing the correct style for a given situation is a matter of accurate judgement. The appropriate decision will vary from context to context and from moment to moment.

Moreover, the choice is never simply either X or Y; it is likely to be a combination of both. Richard Koch refers to 'Theory Y' managers as 'liberating' managers: "There is nothing soft about being a liberating manager. It demands high rather than low standards. A performance culture without liberation is a pity, but a liberating culture without performance is unsustainable."

It is not so much a dilemma as a paradox. How can you be a liberating manager and be a demanding one at the same time?

In my grandfather's time, his managers could apply a 'command and control' style. They didn't need to do anything other than rule by fear. They held Granddad's life, and that of every member of his family, in their hands. If they chose to finish him, he lost everything. As a mineworker, his house, heating, education, everything was tied to his job. If he lost one, he lost all.

Fortunately, times have changed. A Chinese proverb says, "You can throw a stone across a river but you can't throw a bird." Birds, like people, have freedom of will and choice. Granddad was deprived of his, as were many of his generation.

The challenges of modern managers are so much greater than they were back then. Now, business leaders and owners have a choice as to whether they are going to inspire by love or rule by fear. Whichever they choose, they need to do it well. If they do it well, they are likely to become the employer of choice; if not, the best staff members will vote with their feet.

We get the team we deserve.

CHAPTER 30

Lynne gently closed her office door at lunchtime, trying not to attract attention from the open sales area. She didn't want to be disturbed during this lunch hour at her desk, yet there'd been so much gossip and post trauma after the rowdy fallout with Fay in her office that she didn't want to invoke any more.

It was time to face the music. Ever since her conversation with Ian, she'd felt a growing need to establish the new way forward with the company as a whole. Although her epiphany had started with a simple decision to change, she'd gradually become convinced, galvanised and truly driven to act on the new way ahead for Erimus Manufacturing's management team. The self-doubt and hesitation that once paralysed her had completely vanished with the arrival of this new sense of conviction – no, passion for the company. No purpose, even.

Nobody else knew it yet, but she did: she was changed. Awoken, lit up.

Lynne looked at the outline of her dim reflection in her computer screen as she logged onto the internet, her salad and sandwich sitting beside it untouched. Did she look different, too?

She smiled as she caught herself thinking like a child and turned to the matter at hand: Erimus needed her to negotiate Fay's involvement in its future.

It was not going to be as simple as leaving it to Fay to decide if or when she wanted to return to work. The shock would come when Lynne explained that she believed that she wasn't a fit for the company and that she shouldn't return. It might start Armageddon.

Oddly, even such a potentially unpleasant prospect of yet another argument with her sister couldn't bring her down. She noted in a strange, detached way how she looked for the humour and hope in the situation as she visited website after website, searching for the right venue for the conversation.

Which restaurant in the city would be dead right for what could develop into a real, sisterly spat?

The trouble was, Lynne was looking for somewhere public to meet her very piqued Little Sis to break the news that she was letting her go.

Screw ambience. Screw menus. Screw service. What Lynne was searching for was a place with witnesses and a quick escape route.

She found the website of a simple, elegant and light restaurant with a wide, open area and a simple menu and made a note of it in her diary. A place with an outside area would be a good bet, she reasoned. Lots of people about to witness a murder if there was one.

She laughed at loud at the thought, making Roxy jump as she walked past her window splashing a mug of coffee. She waved, and Roxy smiled back, wondering if Lynne was finally cracking up.

How could she feel so calm about it all? When you know that you know you're doing the right thing, she thought, you have peace of mind.

Conviction brings peace. She jotted that down in her diary, too, and then opened her mailbox to compose her sister's invitation to lunch.

At ten past one on the appointed day, Lynne sat people-watching at her table-for-two in "La Maison", a light, breezy space on the ground floor of one of Middlesbrough's most impressive malls. The restaurant had an opening onto to the concourse, full of sunlight as it poured in through the glass roof and sparkled off an indoor fountain surrounded by fresh, rich ferns and trailing plants.

Shoppers milled around contentedly, eating ice creams in the welcome warmth and inspecting their bags full of new buys. At the tables closer to her, Lynne watched a couple chat animatedly, smiling into each other's eyes and sipping their way lingeringly through a bottle of Chateauneuf du Pape. Crisp white table linen and little glass vases holding primroses added a delicate hint of Spring, bringing the onset of newness of life and refreshment from the outside in.

It had been a good choice, Lynne felt, and on any other day she'd be content to sit there like this for a few hours. Today, though, all her peaceful feelings and happy thoughts of late had abandoned her, leaving her to face Fay with not much more than a plan of how she wanted the conversation to flow and a complete loss of appetite.

She took a deep breath and tried to slow her heart rate – a trick she first tried to master when she was a child. What a bloody ridiculous thing to try to do, she thought. Nobody can slow their heart by concentrating on it; whenever she concentrated on hers it would get completely self-conscious and beat all the faster, as though she'd just caught it slacking off at work or something.

Fay was already ten minutes late. This was to be expected, punctuality had never been one of her strengths – well, not until Ian had insisted every Tuesday at twelve - but her lateness was not so easily suffered this time. Every minute dragged by. Lynne hoped that she wouldn't appear too nervous when her sister arrived, as that would put her on the defence. A defensive Fay was a volatile Fay, and irrespective of Lynne's careful choice of a public space she wasn't certain that it could contain the full force if she blew.

She arrived in a swirl of flowery cotton and cloud of perfume, turning heads and commanding the attention of the whole mall, it seemed, until she sat down opposite her sister, placing her clutch bag on the table next to her setting.

"You look summery," Lynne offered.

"Thank you. I like to make the most of my casual wardrobe while I'm on leave," Fay patted her hair and looked around her for an audience but nobody was paying attention.

Lynne chose not to take the bait: Fay was not on leave. She was AWOL and any other employee would be facing disciplinary for it, not being taken out for lunch. She smiled briefly as the waitress filled their glasses with sparkling mineral water and handed them menus.

Lynne recalled the conversations she'd had with Ian. He had pressed her to make a decision about Fay, the family and the business. When Lynne was clear on her priorities and they had spoken about how she should conduct this lunchtime meeting, he repeated another of his mantras:

"It's important to begin with the end in mind, Lynne" he had asserted. "Decide on the outcomes you want from the meeting and then reverse engineer the process to lead to those outcomes".

It was a long and personally painful conversation. Could Fay convince Lynne of her willingness and ability to become an 'A-Player' and a manager worthy of a place on Erimus' new leadership team? Could she put the business and its stakeholders first? If not, she would have to leave the company. Lynne realised that this was indeed a crucial conversation and she was determined to do the right thing and execute the plan successfully.

She wasted no time in getting to the point.

"I'm glad we could meet up. We need to sort this out, Fay."

Her sister looked serious for a moment and contrived to sound adult.

"I know. We sisters need to present a united front at work. Which is why I was so upset that you undermined me by firing one of my staff without discussing it with me. Mother was shocked when she heard about it."

From whom, though? Lynne let this one go, too, concentrating as she'd promised herself she would to keep her eye on the ball and keep this a business and business-like exchange. She waited for her sister to finish with her menu and call the attention of the waitress to order for them both before she continued.

"You see, I don't want the fact that we're sisters to be influence our behaviour as fellow managers in Erimus at all. Or that either of our parents were involved before us, come to that. I can see that all it's doing is confusing the business issues and holding all of us back from moving forward in the professional and appropriate way our team wants needs and deserves. Can you see that?"

Fay raised her glass to her lips and gazed at Lynne over the rim, eyes as round as an owl's. Of course, the family had to come into it. For her part, it was her winning card when it came to her negotiating her way at work. What on earth was she talking about?

"Oh, I couldn't possible agree with you on that one, sis," she tittered. "The company is the family – it's always been that way. No family, no Erimus Manufacturing. That's what Dad always used to say, anyway. What would he think if he heard you say that?"

Lynne was sure that he'd think quite a lot, but she still held on to the reins of the conversation and would not be swayed. She stuck to her plan, her agenda and the business of the business. This time, emotional blackmail would not work.

"That's just it. It used to be the way. The old way – part of the 'command and control' regime," she explained. "But it's not our way now. Now, we need to be better than that. We have started to become much better than that and I realise that we can't go back to those old ways. Erimus has changed fundamentally, and Fay -"

She folded her hands together in front of her, keeping them steady and leaning in to the table, matching her sister's stare unblinking.

"- if you can't change, too, then you're not a fit with the company."

The chatter and clinking surrounding their table seemed to fade to dull silence as Fay looked at her sister in utter disbelief. As she sat staring at Lynne, holding her glass suspended in mid-air and her mouth still half full of unswallowed water, she replayed Lynne's last statement at least four times in her head.

Lynne made a point of not glancing at the glass but meeting Fay's stare full on. This was the moment of decision: they both sensed it. Which reaction would Fay choose? To create a full-blown drama and its ensuing chaos, or to behave like an adult and see reason for once? Lynne wasn't particularly religious, but she silently said a quick prayer right then.

The waitress broke the silence as she approached their table with their dishes, oblivious to the tension that fizzed between them. Fay's astonished gaze was drawn to her plate, and Lynne leapt at her chance the natural break had presented.

"Fay, you've been a part of the transformation in the leadership team since it began several weeks ago. You've seen with your own eyes how the new way of working together, the values and the systems that have been put in place to affect really good change have affected everyone – from the leadership team right down through the company.

"People are really pulling together, enjoying being part of the business and as a result the results are transforming themselves. There is no place for anyone who doesn't want to operate in that way now," Lynne said firmly, appealing to her sister. "And no place for family perks, special treatment and nepotism, either. Erimus is no longer a family-run business in the old, traditional sense. It has to be managed in the most professional way possible. Being a family member bestows no privileges anymore."

Images of Andrew, Roxy and Natalie laughing in the management meetings and Ian handing out his WWW forms flashed across Fay's mind. It was true, she thought; things were no longer done simply because she or Lynne demanded them to be done. They were discussed, debated, decided and driven forwards and taken care of by the team as a whole, and she'd always felt like the outsider. She'd never be one of them on that level; she simply wasn't a team player and had no desire to be.

Growing up in the Peston family had been traumatic, shifting and unpredictable; it had led to her developing an inescapable defence system of self-isolation and mistrust in others. Fay couldn't help feeling that she would be better running her own show, making her own choices and just telling other people what to think and what to do. That way she wouldn't feel jealous of or threatened by anybody. The way it always used to be. Why did it have to change? But of course, she could see that it did.

She looked up at Lynne, who was still waiting for her response.

"I'm not the only one who isn't a natural team player," she accused her. Lynne could see now where her thoughts had led her. "You grew up in the same home as me, remember! How come you're so hot on all this change suddenly? What makes you so likely to embrace a different style?"

Her voice was lifting in volume and pitch, and Lynne braced herself against an impending storm. She looked at her sister and understood the hurt behind her defiant expression; in the spirit of the new core values, she chose the honest response.

"You're right. I'm not an expert. Far from it. The difference is that I have thought long and hard about this and I know I have to change. The company and the people deserve it. I know it will be very hard to do and so I'm committing to intensive one to one coaching and maybe even personal therapy, too. I need understand my own responses and to learn how to deal with my management responsibilities and reactions in a way that will allow everyone else in the company to grow."

Really? She'd go through all of that just for her job? Fay looked at her sister and suddenly saw a real desire to change.

"It's the only way I can be sure they have a chance to fulfil their potential as individuals and that the business can achieve what it needs to achieve. We simply can't survive in the twenty-first century with the same style that worked fifty years ago. It's going to be a hard change for me. I'm feeling extremely daunted by it, to be honest. And Fay, you'd need to shift massively, too, were you to stay. It's the only way you'd be able to become the branch manager we need. Are you willing to make that sort of sacrifice?"

Lynne was serious, Fay could sense it. She tried to picture herself having endless one to one coaching sessions, group coaching with the team, constant battles with a changing staff complement. Then she imagined the never-ending arguments with her parents because things weren't being done the way her father would have done them – and she realised she didn't have the stomach for it. She backed down.

"No," she said, quietly. "No, I don't have either the desire or the energy for it all."

The sisters regarded each other as the seconds ticked by, each caught in a flurry of flashbacks – first as the best of childhood friends, then as the worst of enemies. So many years of misunderstanding and rivalry mixed in with support, co-dependency and even love. The tension dissipated. The best decision had, at last, been made.

Lynne smiled, reached for Fay's hand and gave it a little squeeze.

"Okay, then," she said, reaching for her cutlery. "Let's get you on your feet doing what you really want to do."

It was going to be a long journey ahead for both of them, she knew. Thank God she'd picked the right restaurant.

CHAPTER 31

From: Lynne Peston

To: Management Team

Subject: Fay Peston

Dear All,

It is with some sadness that I must report that Fay is leaving the company to follow other career opportunities. Fay has been a part of Erimus Manufacturing for as long as I have, and has done much to further the Middlesbrough branch and to grow its reputation in the North East.

I know that we will all miss her and we wish her every success in the next step of her working life.

Please join me in the boardroom at 4:00pm this afternoon for an important briefing.

With thanks,

Lynne

Roxy and Natalie opened the email at the same time, just a few seconds after Lynne hit the 'Send' button. They read it in shock, each looking up automatically at the end of it to see what the other was thinking.

"Oh, boy," breathed Roxy, looking around for Andrew and wondering if he'd picked it up on his mobile yet. What would he think? They'd have to find a new branch manager, now.

Natalie leapt one step ahead. Lynne's already found somebody to replace her, she thought. That's probably what this afternoon's meeting is going to be about. She stared with her mouth open at Roxy's shocked face for a few seconds before quietly standing and moving towards the kitchen to make coffee for them both. It was vital that none of the sales team in the office registered that something was up before the management team had had a chance to discuss it.

As she added the milk, she wondered what Fay would do next. Indeed, who would employ her.

Everyone was in the boardroom a clear ten minutes before Lynne walked in. So far, none of them had talked about the email.

It's odd, Andrew thought, as he watched Lynne take her seat at the head of the table. In the old days, the gossip would have been flying around the office like a swarm of killer bees, and everybody from the top rung down would have heard the 'confidential' news and come up with their own dramatic version of what had been said to whom, by whom, where and exactly when.

The gossiping, backbiting and bitchy comments had reduced dramatically over recent weeks as they had all started to know and respect each other more. It couldn't all be down to Fay's absence.

This time, it was clear that none of the managers had talked at all. Not even to each other. Andrew was taken aback at just how muted he felt and wondered if they all felt the same, conflicting feelings.

Fay was not popular in the office, it was true. She was bitchy, self-absorbed, headstrong and often unfair to her staff; she blamed others for shared mistakes, picking on a scapegoat and bullying him or her for weeks. She could be a right pain the ass, but she was their pain in the ass. Lately, she had seemed to soften and change, at least during the management meetings, and he'd held out for a day when they could even have a one-to-one without her sneering at the very thought of it.

Now, there was no hope of that. Somebody new was going to take her place, and that was going to change their team in ways that he couldn't imagine. Did Lynne already have someone in mind? It would be just typical of her to shoot from the hip without consulting anyone else – firing her sister and targeting an unsuspecting incumbent with the same bullet.

"Afternoon, everyone," Lynne shuffled her ledger and papers around in front of her. Her hand shook a little, but she held her smile.

Natalie answered for them, as the others were too tense to open their mouths.

"I have a couple of news items to tell you in what will have to be a very brief meeting now," Lynne started, "and the first is Fay, of course."

She looked around at their faces, the afternoon sunshine lighting up their expressions of apprehension. They look like kids in a nursery listening to a storybook, the thought tickled. She allowed herself the briefest of moments to allow it into her imagination, seeing them all – herself included – as four year olds together, learning how to get on nicely. She smiled, and hugged the feeling of warmth and excitement she'd been trying to cover up ever since lunchtime.

"Fay and I had a meeting recently," she remembered the restaurant and the tension she'd felt in such a lovely place, "and we talked properly. Mostly about how the company has changed direction and where we're going as a team from now on, how we behave, and how we work together," she picked her words and slowed her speech on purpose. "I am so proud of what we have accomplished already as a team. I think every one of us would have to agree that there have been massive improvements and that there are big changes ahead still. Am I right?"

They all nodded, easing a little in their chairs in response to the unusual warmth in her tone.

She kept eye contact with each of them, speaking from the heart. "Fay and I discussed these changes and she honoured us all by being frank with me that she feels that it's time for her to move on. She no longer feels the right 'fit' for the company in the light of our new style, and I agreed with her. She has submitted her resignation, which I've accepted, and she's left us with huge love and best wishes for the future."

They all looked away from her at this point, assimilating the news and feeling suddenly nostalgic for someone they'd always wished at the bottom of a well. Human nature is funny, Lynne thought, but knew exactly how they felt.

"Of course," she continued, "it means she'll need to be replaced. I would like to go about the recruitment differently this time and we'll have a proper meeting together to discuss the process and the role. I would value your input in adding to the Senior Leadership Team."

Andrew looked up. So, she hadn't already recruited someone? She was actually going to ask the rest of the team for input? He blinked, not quite recognising her for a second or two.

Natalie suddenly exhaled loudly and slumped back in her chair.

"So, what's the big news, then?" she blurted, and the rest laughed. She blushed and kicked herself under the table. "I mean, I'm so glad Fay's okay ..."

Lynne deflected the group's attention from her agony.

"The big news is ... I've heard back from Stadia UK Developments."

She turned to look at Andrew, whose face suddenly slackened, focusing on her gaze and her next words. Nothing else rooted him to the ground: this is what it must feel like to be in space, he thought.

A huge grin found her face before she could find her voice. "We've got it."

As the others leapt to their feet, shrieking in unison and rushing to hug her and each other, he sat, stunned.

Lynne watched him, laughing as Natalie thumped her on the back, and mouthed a silent message:

"Thank you."

My God. We are a real team, now, he thought, and slowly climbed to his feet to join in.

CHAPTER 32

The Awards Night was the one night of the year that business owners and community leaders could count on rubbing shoulders with their top competition, colleagues and friends – each making the most of the opportunity to network, relax a little and gossip. The sounds of glasses clinking, dance music drifting in through the large, swing doors to the dining area and the sparkling glimmers from the heavy ceiling chandeliers filled the large reception with a sense of celebration.

Lynne shifted uncomfortably, feeling held in by her dress and lamed by her shoes, trying to focus on the glamourous guests milling around her.

"Penny for your thoughts," Andrew appeared at her left shoulder bearing a glass of champagne.

Lynne took her glass with thanks and raised it to his, looking around the room now filling up with the great and the good from all over the North of England for the Annual Regional Business Awards.

The room was buzzing with excitement ahead of the awards ceremony. As they waited to enter the main hall for the banquet and prize giving, the team from Erimus Manufacturing mingled with colleagues, clients and competitors, everybody sparkling and at their finest.

From where she stood, Lynne could see Roxy and Natalie chatting with the mayor of Darlington, both transformed in their gowns and turning heads. She felt a rush of pride for them; nobody would guess that they'd just come through an unprecedented three weeks of hard slog and overtime.

Still, it had all been worth it.

The happy crowd migrated to the main hall, where the dressed tables lit up the space. Candelabras, crystal glasses, original centrepieces with ostrich feathers and flowers, and the wide stage ready for all the evening's accolades from the podium.

It was a sight; a fitting occasion for the winners-in-waiting for their hard work over the past year.

Lynne didn't mind if they didn't win their category. The news of their nomination had come as the cherry on the top of an unforgettable, three-month journey for her team, and nothing could detract from the glow of their winning the Stadia UK Developments contract. It meant that there was a huge amount of work to do, decisions to be made regarding recruiting and outsourcing, planning and endless amounts of paperwork - but all for the good.

The Middlesbrough branch was safe. Nobody on the team had ever suspected that it wasn't, but she'd never forget the stress and the sleepless nights that led to her making the audacious, desperate pitch that paid off, against all odds. Tonight, they would celebrate altogether. They could get back to work tomorrow.

She took her place at the company table in the middle of the room, taking in the surrounding chatter and music and thinking that her little crowd scrubbed up pretty well, holding their own in the prestigious gathering.

A couple of tables away, Ian had a moment's respite from the well-wishers and meaningless small talk with friends and acquaintances and looked around, getting his bearings. He spotted the Erimus Manufacturing team, laughing together, enjoying the evening. Even Lynne was glowing with warmth and the attractiveness he'd noticed that day at the Peston stables when she talked so animatedly about her riding.

How that group had changed. Each one of them was developing, growing as both an individual and collectively as a synergised team. Their recent success was well-deserved, although there was still a lot of improvement needed to carry out the task ahead of them, professionally and profitably and still continue to grow the business. Still, they had made a solid start by becoming a cohesive team, with more rigorous management processes, a common purpose, core values and an upward trajectory.

Three days ago, on Tuesday at twelve, he'd visited them for follow up. The offices were still sparkling, and the meeting rooms upstairs now sported shiny signs on their doors, each bearing the name of one of their new core values: Care, Empathy and Honesty. As he sat with them, the meeting started with a review of the previous week's WWW as usual but there had been an addition to the three-point agenda since Ian had last attended.

In turn, everyone stood up and shared an anecdote of how one or other of their core values had been demonstrated in the preceding week, either by themselves or by a member of their team. It was certainly effective at keeping the core values alive in the business and the focus of attention. Ian was impressed. The atmosphere in the whole building was positive and happy, with the staff going about their work with smiles on their faces.

After the meeting, Lynne had asked him to continue his work with them as a leadership team on a regular rhythm and he'd happily accepted – but only on the condition that Lynne committed to personal coaching herself at the same time. She had come a long way already but still had a long way to go; she would need to grow even more quickly as the business began to scale up.

He smiled at the thought of their success and imagined the new stadium in all its glory, bringing prestige and growth to the North East.

Andrew took a large gulp of champagne and tried to relax. He felt out of his element in this sort of environment; a part of him wished he were flat out on his sofa listening to *AC/DC*. Looking around his table, though, he felt that he was among friends. Natalie, Roxy and Lynne were laughing together as though they were joined at the hip, and Pete was having great fun taking endless videos that were bound to end up on his Twitter feed before the end of the night.

He saw Ian sitting close by and gave him a big smile. He was a part of the Erimus team now, too, he felt. They all did.

The only thing that threatened to spoil their evening was the empty place next to him, where Fay should have been sitting. They hadn't seen or heard from her for three weeks now – ever since she'd left after the row with Lynne. Of course, Fay was moving on from the company but she had played an intrinsic part in the team and had been invited to join them all tonight. He glanced at Lynne now, wondering how much the empty chair was spoiling her evening. From the looks of it, not much. It was good to see her enjoying herself, but still ... he couldn't imagine that she didn't miss her sister.

As the starter course was served, the hubbub dwindled and the MC for the night mounted the stage, quietly checking his script and repositioning his microphone. Roxy nudged Natalie in anticipation; close together, they watched as the house lights dimmed and the spotlight fell on him.

"Good evening, ladies and gentlemen," he began, and the audience clapped and whistled, excited to hear who had won what.

One by one, he read out the nominees for each category and the winners emerged in their teams from all around the room to cheers and music to collect their trophies. To have a Regional Business Award in the office was a huge accolade and always triggered a year's worth of press coverage and lucrative networking opportunities.

Roxy looked at Andrew and knew what he was thinking: wouldn't it be great to have one of those at Erimus Manufacturing?

Lynne was distracted. She checked her phone for the time: 8:50 pm. She frowned and looked towards the entrance. Come on, Fay, she willed. What's the hold up?

She caught Ian's questioning look in her line of vision and smiled. She must just relax, she told herself, breathing deeply and turning back to her table. Have a little faith, girl.

The awards moved on through the second course. They were getting close to the main categories, now, and the already awarded trophies glittered on the tables of the lucky winners, all drinking with more abandon now that their moment in the spotlight was mercifully over.

Erimus Manufacturing had been nominated along with three other companies for the "Fast Growth Business Award". The other three contenders were much younger companies and so Andrew didn't really rate their chances. Still, it was an honour to be recognised with the nomination. He chatted amiably with Pete as their second courses arrived – delicious roast duck, fresh vegetables and the obligatory trough of Yorkshire puddings for the table to share.

Suddenly, Natalie let out a yell. Andrew dropped his knife in surprise and by the time he'd picked it up from the floor, everyone at his table was standing up, hugging and fussing over a very elegant Fay.

Lynne smiled from ear to ear, clearly genuinely happy as she waited for her sister to disengage herself from Roxy's arms and turn to her.

"Hey, little Sis," she said softly, and Fay responded by giving her a warm, long hug and a kiss on the cheek.

Over the last three weeks, the only thing that had marred the newfound excitement at Erimus Manufacturing was the continuing rift between the two sisters. Or, she should say, the Group Managing Director and the Middlesbrough Branch Manager.

Lynne had taken to heart her discussion with Ian and had acted positively. She knew that she needed to speak with Fay candidly, not in their father's style, but in her own: with care, empathy and honesty and at the same time separating the needs of the business from the loyalties of family.

Their lunch meeting had been long. There'd been some recriminations on Fay's part, but Lynne remembered Ian's advice and stuck rigidly to the subject of the company's welfare, leaving the family's issues to one side.

They'd left the restaurant as sisters, but no longer colleagues; and with Fay's promise that she'd wear her new Chanel gown to the Regional Business Awards Night.

"And now for the nominees of the 'Fast Growth Business Award'," the MC's voice interrupted the celebrations at the table. Fay grabbed Lynne's hand and squeezed it hard, smiling and crossing her fingers for the others to see.

Ian saw, too. Well, well. Who'd have thought those two would ever be on the same side, supporting each other? He could hardly believe his eyes. Ian realised that now that Fay was no longer a part of the business and the management team, her natural love of and support for her sister could be expressed fully and joyfully. Being able to separate the business and the family had been a necessary if hard-won victory. Lynne's father's negative influence might take longer to fully exorcise, mind you.

"Erimus Manufacturing!" The announcement of the winner boomed from the PA and the room immediately erupted into applause and cheers.

The team froze for a second, looking at each other in disbelief and amazement.

"Come on, everyone," said Lynne, taking charge. "It's our time."

They rose as one, threading their way around the tables in front of them towards the stage. Lynne grabbed Fay's hand and led her in a detour past Ian's table.

He beamed at them, a little misty-eyed.

"Thank you," she said, and planted a kiss on his cheek.

Later, as the lights gradually dimmed and the music grew louder, Lynne watched with satisfaction as the energy in the room swelled, welcoming the fresh promise of a party.

People began to push their chairs back, stand up and mingle with their colleagues at the tables closest to their own; glasses were recharged and laughter sprinkled the top notes of the music. Within seconds, excited winners began to drop their guard and run across the room to find their friends to share their triumphs. The sudden movement and increase in pace triggered the first small group to the dancefloor; as the ice was broken more followed, driven on by each other's company and moving between the darting coloured lights.

It was a good feeling. To Lynne, it was a sense of resolution in itself – the celebration at the end of a difficult chapter. She allowed herself a mental pat on the back, laughing as she saw Roxy drag an awkward Andrew into the middle of the now busy dancefloor, whooping and raising her arms above her head as she moved in time to the kind of music that Andrew certainly didn't own on vinyl. He self-consciously shuffled about to show willing, but Lynne could see he was rather pleased.

By now she was the only one still at their table, the others having migrated to different areas in the room to catch up with industry colleagues they rarely saw. Brendan Tucker from Millsurge Holdings caught her eye, smiled and clapped his hands together towards her in congratulations. She gave him a wide smile and mouthed 'thank you', all the while struggling to hold back the urge to leap up from her chair and punch the air with excitement.

What a difference a few months makes, she thought. What a difference having a team that's pulling together makes, come to that. She glanced around for the man who'd helped to turn things around for Erimus Manufacturing; if she could find him, now would be a good time to thank him. She grabbed her bag and dug around for her compact and lipstick, applying a quick touch-up as most of hers had somehow ended up all around the rims of three champagne flutes.

Ian was silhouetted in the main doorway of the hall, the foyer behind him lit up with busy networkers and gossiping partners. He was talking to two men that Lynne didn't know, and as she approached the little group she hesitated, not wanting to interrupt them.

"This, gentlemen, is the young lady I was telling you about," Ian grinned at her, gesturing her to come forward and join their conversation. "Lynne, meet Matt Gordon, CEO of Indie Enterprises and George Scorey, Managing Director of Europa Shipping."

Lynne smiled and shook their hands, grateful to be introduced so readily and conversationally by Ian, who sold her up so well she almost didn't recognise herself in his description. She blushed slightly but held her head up, thanking him and saying a quick prayer of thanks for the low lighting. She needn't have worried, though; the two strangers were as relaxed as Ian and she quickly found herself totally absorbed in the chat, cracking a couple of jokes and feeling at home with them.

That was it: I'm feeling at home, she thought. That was the feeling that made tonight so different. I really do belong here, and this time I haven't had to try too hard. And it's not just that I belong in this room: I belong to a team. My God – I had to break with the 'family' out of the business to create a real feeling of family within the business.

The thought made her laugh, fortunately at an appropriate moment in the conversation, and she was rewarded with a slightly overlong look of admiration from the CEO of Indie Enterprises.

Ian came to her rescue.

"If you'll excuse us," he said, lightly touching Lynne's elbow, "Lynne and I need to have a quick catch up. I'll be in touch next week."

They nodded their farewells and he guided her through the main doors and out into the foyer, grabbing them each a glass of champagne from a passing waiter as he glided past them, serving tray aloft.

"What? More champagne?" She laughed but didn't protest when he handed one to her.

"Well, there's a lot to celebrate after all," he smiled and raised his glass to hers with a congratulatory clink. "I'm so pleased for you. You've achieved so much – first the big deal, now this award. Where's it going to go?"

She hadn't thought about that. It would be the first award they'd won, and in her mind's eye she could see a whole array of them covering the walls, just like some mega music management office with platinum discs hanging everywhere.

"Reception," she decided firmly. "Our visitors should be greeted with a bit of bling when they walk in the door. And until all the others are won we'll fill up the gaps with big, leafy plants and a shiny new café area ..."

Ian laughed as he watched her mind visualising it all as she gazed into middle distance.

"There's no reason why you shouldn't have as many as you like there – it's a great idea."

"Testimonials, too ..." Lynne murmured, eyes half closed with a smile.

Ian allowed her a moment to enjoy the bright, mental picture, only speaking when she seemed to come back to the moment and the re-join the hubbub in the foyer.

"You know, it's going to take as much work from now on as it has so far," he started. Should he go easy on her now? Underplay the challenges he could see looming in her company's near future?

Hell, no. She could take it. And she deserved the truth.

She raised an eyebrow at him, giving her face a mixed expression of curiosity and distrust. Like a pigeon eying up crusty piece of bread, he thought idly, as he waited for her response.

"Sure – it'll take commitment to keep up this momentum," she assured him, "but we know what we're doing now, thanks to you. I can't thank you enough for your help, Ian, really. You've been bloody great."

Ah, there it was. The moment Ian had been expecting. The assumption that Lynne now knew everything she needed to know. The sign off. The end of term feeling - it's all done with, now. Sorted. Probably the most dangerous time for any growth company or management team.

"It's been a pleasure," Ian said, quickly dismissing the memories of the times that had been anything but a pleasure. "But it's not over yet. Lynne, you particularly are going to need support, strength, flexibility and a whole new skill set to take your company to the next level. Some of the basics are now in place, certainly, but speaking from my experience, you are about to meet new challenges that you have never had to face before. As Erimus scales up it will become exponentially more complex. You will inevitably face bigger challenges than you have done already. The best thing you can do is make sure you have the attitude, skills and knowledge to deal with them."

He ushered her to a couple of armchairs that had become available and they sat, each privately braced for a profound exchange. He spoke carefully but firmly.

"Tonight, and perhaps for the next couple of weeks, all is well with the team. But you know that in a team structure there is no such thing as a steady state," Ian went on. "Sooner rather than later, the new dynamic you're enjoying now will shift; remember the four stages – 'forming', 'storming', 'norming' and 'performing'?"

Lynne nodded, with a growing feeling that he was about to give her some bad news.

"Well, guess which one is likely to come next?"

She groaned and rolled her eyes. "Probably storming," she pouted.

"Correct. And at that point, you need to be better equipped than you are right now to deal with the new situation – whatever it's going to be. Think about it: what's the next big, obvious thing you're going to have to do that is likely to change the dynamic of your management team?"

"Replace Fay."

That was a no-brainer. She'd been secretly troubled about that since her conversation with her sister regarding her future with the company.

"Recruiting the right person is going to be a new challenge for you and the team. You will need to find someone who not only matches your core values but also someone who is of sufficient calibre for the way the company is now and will be in the future. You can't employ people who are 'smaller' than you are if you want the company to continue to grow, so you will have to grow to be the leader they deserve."

Ian paused for a moment to let this sink in. "Not to mention the fact that the introduction of anyone new to a group changes the dynamic inherently, right away. The higher calibre the team, the greater the expectations they have of the leader."

Lynne could see that, and tried to picture the team's progress once the new branch manager was in place. It was all a blur and a bit frightening.

Talk about a mood-changer. As if on-cue, the music sank from bouncy pop to a slow dance. Marvin Gaye, *'Let's Get It On'*.

Hey, let's not, she thought.

She shook her head, feeling the old sensation of defensive irritation start in the pit of her stomach again. How dare he rain on her parade, tonight of all nights? Couldn't she just have one moment off from all this training hype? For God's sake. The bloke had no feelings, no sense of occasion. Rude git.

She swigged back the rest of her champagne in one gulp, and was about to stagger to her feet and end the conversation when she saw Roxy and Andrew through the open doors on the dancefloor, swaying toe-to-toe in a very friendly way.

Ian followed her astonished stare.

"And what if those two 'get it on'?" he couldn't resist asking. "What's your policy on relationships at work? How will you handle that one?"

She blushed properly this time and looked away from them, just as Andrew was apologising profusely for standing on Roxy's foot, and she was laughing and pretending to be cross. Lynne realised this journey that the team were taking and that she had eventually joined them on might have a beginning but probably didn't have an end.

"You've cleared the first hurdle brilliantly, Lynne," Ian soothed her. "But it was only the first hurdle. There are many more to come." Secretly, he was more concerned about her slipping back into her old 'command-and-control' style of management. Old habits die hard, and that one would destroy all the good they'd achieved so far, if it were allowed to. She needed personal coaching, and plenty of it.

Lynne looked up directly into his eyes. He was right again. Dammit.

"We need to continue with the leadership team coaching," she offered eventually. Then, "I need more coaching. One to one. Can you continue to help us? Me?"

Ian smiled at her, held out his hand. She took it, and he helped her to her feet.

"With pleasure," he said, and breathed a sigh of relief. Then, in a voice that only she could hear: "To your success."

INDEX

A

accident	- 97 -, - 98 -, - 107 -, - 108 -, - 122 -, - 153 -, - 174 -
accountability	- 79 -, - 102 -, - 109 -, - 131 -, - 132 -, - 133 -, - 139 -, - 210 -
accountant	- 53 -
accounts	- 71 -, - 78 -, - 116 -, - 124 -, - 187 -
admin	- 35 -, - 64 -, - 78 -, - 105 -, - 106 -
agenda	- 22 -, - 53 -, - 55 -, - 56 -, - 121 -, - 135 -
agreement	- 143 -, - 146 -, - 172 -
alignment	- 63 -
A-Player Grid	- 197 -
appraisal	- 192 -, - 193 -, - 197 -
atmosphere	- 26 -, - 53 -, - 105 -, - 121 -, - 145 -, - 146 -, - 170 -, - 283 -
attend	- 55 -, - 121 -, - 224 -, - 225 -, - 240 -
attendance	- 50 -
attendees	- 56 -
authentic	- 258 -
autonomy	- 87 -, - 89 -, - 92 -, - 147 -, - 171 -, - 197 -
awareness	- 100 -, - 101 -, - 102 -

B

beliefs	- 177 -
Black Bag Day	- 226 -
blame	- 131 -, - 132 -, - 133 -
boardroom	- 18 -, - 36 -, - 49 -, - 58 -, - 61 -, - 70 -, - 71 -, - 74 -, - 79 -, - 83 -, - 84 -, - 85 -, - 105 -, - 120 -, - 134 -, - 152 -, - 180 -, - 238 -, - 241 -, - 242 -, - 248 -
Boss	- 22 -
bottom line	- 119 -, - 159 -
branches	- 16 -, - 23 -
briefs	- 39 -

business leaders — 15 -, - 261 -, - 262 -

C

care — 19 -, - 48 -, - 149 -, - 151 -, - 179 -, - 198 -, - 256 -, - 257 -, - 259 -, - 286 -
cause and effect — 131 -
CEO — 17 -
challenge — 73 -, - 130 -, - 135 -, - 144 -, - 149 -, - 154 -, - 168 -, - 200 -, - 226 -, - 261 -
clarity — 55 -
client — 101 -, - 124 -, - 125 -, - 128 -, - 139 -, - 185 -, - 186 -, - 193 -
clients — 19 -, - 20 -, - 124 -, - 153 -, - 256 -, - 281 -
coaching — 139 -, - 185 -, - 188 -, - 191 -, - 192 -, - 211 -, - 283 -
colleagues — 17 -, - 83 -, - 152 -, - 180 -, - 183 -, - 186 -, - 281 -, - 286 -
command and control — 15 -, - 252 -, - 255 -, - 261 -, - 262 -
commentary — 169 -
COMMENTARY: MEETING MUSTS — 54 -
commitment — 16 -, - 192 -
communicate — 48 -, - 67 -, - 163 -
community — 16 -, - 155 -, - 259 -
company - 12 -, - 15 -, - 16 -, - 17 -, - 20 -, - 23 -, - 25 -, - 28 -, - 29 -, - 34 -, - 38 -, - 40 -, - 41 -, - 49 -, - 65 -, - 67 -, - 98 -, - 107 -, - 108 -, - 114 -, - 115 -, - 128 -, - 129 -, - 134 -, - 135 -, - 136 -, - 153 -, - 174 -, - 187 -, - 191 -, - 193 -, - 197 -, - 198 -, - 203 -, - 215 -, - 218 -, - 245 -, - 252 -, - 254 -, - 255 -, - 256 -, - 258 -, - 282 -, - 286 -
competition — 13 -, - 41 -, - 131 -, - 224 -
conflict — 73 -
consistency — 55 -
contribute — 171 -
contribution — 92 -
core values — 80 -, - 115 -, - 160 -, - 169 -, - 174 -, - 175 -, - 177 -, - 178 -, - 179 -, - 194 -, - 196 -, - 197 -, - 199 -, - 200 -, - 201 -, - 202 -, - 254 -, - 255 -, - 256 -, - 257 -, - 258 -, - 282 -
C-Player — 198 -, - 202 -
creative — 34 -
culture of the business — 202 -

D

David Taylor — 139 -
decision — 22 -, - 24 -, - 131 -, - 159 -, - 178 -, - 184 -, - 188 -, - 201 -, - 210 -, - 211 -, - 261 -
Department — 18 -, - 106 -
development — 95 -, - 191 -
direction — 41 -, - 43 -, - 96 -, - 144 -, - 171 -, - 178 -, - 191 -, - 195 -, - 198 -
directors — 17 -, - 20 -, - 23 -

domineering — 29 -, - 64 -, - 100 -
Douglas McGregor — 261 -

E

economic factors — 16 -
email — 37 -, - 51 -, - 59 -, - 146 -, - 149 -, - 171 -, - 193 -, - 206 -, - 225 -, - 243 -, - 248 -
empathy — 163 -, - 253 -, - 256 -, - 257 -, - 286 -
energy — 53 -, - 88 -, - 96 -, - 104 -, - 130 -, - 239 -
environment — 56 -, - 283 -
Erimus - 13 -, - 15 -, - 17 -, - 32 -, - 35 -, - 45 -, - 49 -, - 65 -, - 114 -, - 151 -, - 169 -, - 170 -, - 185 -, - 186 -, - 190 -, - 191 -, - 192 -, - 204 -, - 245 -, - 254 -, - 257 -, - 259 -, - 281 -, - 282 -, - 284 -, - 285 -, - 286 -, - 287 -
exit — 17 -, - 117 -, - 201 -

F

fable of Johnny and Jimmy — 211 -, - 212 -
family — 13 -, - 15 -, - 16 -, - 20 -, - 22 -, - 26 -, - 27 -, - 31 -, - 33 -, - 153 -, - 155 -, - 161 -, - 169 -, - 203 -, - 211 -, - 254 -, - 258 -, - 259 -, - 260 -, - 262 -, - 286 -
fear — 127 -, - 178 -, - 180 -, - 252 -, - 253 -, - 262 -
feedback — 67 -, - 161 -, - 240 -, - 256 -
figures - 20 -, - 23 -, - 35 -, - 47 -, - 53 -, - 62 -, - 63 -, - 64 -, - 65 -, - 67 -, - 74 -, - 75 -, - 77 -, - 78 -, - 79 -, - 106 -, - 112 -, - 115 -, - 118 -, - 120 -, - 121 -, - 123 -, - 124 -, - 128 -, - 134 -, - 137 -, - 143 -, - 147 -, - 172 -, - 182 -, - 184 -, - 185 -, - 241 -, - 243 -, - 244 -
finish time — 56 -
flagship branch — 17 -, - 22 -
forecast — 23 -, - 118 -, - 125 -, - 134 -, - 137 -, - 154 -, - 173 -, - 184 -, - 244 -
form — 64 -, - 92 -, - 121 -, - 129 -, - 146 -, - 148 -, - 188 -, - 200 -
forming — 61 -, - 73 -, - 80 -, - 121 -
four stages — 73 -, - 80 -, - 169 -
Four Stages of Group Development — 80 -
framework — 194 -, - 213 -
freedom — 87 -, - 262 -

G

goals — 100 -
golden rule — 55 -
group dynamics — 73 -, - 169 -
Group Managing Director — 17 -, - 21 -, - 24 -, - 31 -, - 286 -

H

habit	- 49 -, - 67 -, - 71 -, - 74 -
Head of Sales	- 35 -, - 52 -, - 106 -, - 115 -
Health and Safety	- 108 -
honesty	- 286 -

I

ideas	- 34 -, - 70 -, - 148 -, - 149 -, - 184 -, - 214 -, - 215 -, - 224 -
incentivise	- 227 -
initiative	- 149 -, - 159 -
invoice	- 63 -, - 124 -
Ironopolis	- 15 -
ironworks	- 15 -

J

Jim Collins	- 199 -

K

key skill	- 57 -

L

leader	- 53 -, - 57 -, - 80 -, - 91 -, - 211 -, - 224 -, - 227 -
liberating manager	- 262 -
light bulb moments	- 101 -
Liked Best/Next Time	- 172 -

M

machinery	- 35 -, - 97 -
management meeting	- 35 -, - 51 -
management style	- 254 -, - 258 -
management team	- 32 -, - 191 -, - 240 -, - 257 -
Managing	- 17 -, - 21 -, - 24 -, - 31 -, - 51 -, - 215 -, - 286 -
manufacturing	- 15 -, - 18 -, - 29 -, - 35 -, - 59 -

Marketing - 34 -, - 40 -
mastery - 88 -, - 89 -, - 91 -, - 92 -
meeting room - 59 -, - 144 -
meetings - 35 -, - 47 -, - 50 -, - 52 -, - 53 -, - 54 -, - 55 -, - 56 -, - 57 -, - 65 -, - 71 -, - 72 -, - 74 -, - 94 -, - 95 -, - 106 -, - 117 -, - 120 -, - 143 -, - 147 -, - 149 -, - 154 -, - 159 -, - 182 -, - 190 -, - 195 -, - 241 -, - 244 -, - 250 -
Middlesbrough - 13 -, - 15 -, - 17 -, - 29 -, - 153 -, - 161 -, - 214 -, - 257 -, - 281 -, - 286 -
motives - 211 -
Myles Downey - 139 -

N

Nancy Kline - 177 -, - 213 -
norming - 73 -, - 74 -, - 80 -
North East - 12 -, - 15 -, - 16 -, - 161 -, - 215 -, - 283 -

O

off-hiring - 128 -
office - 17 -, - 18 -, - 19 -, - 20 -, - 21 -, - 25 -, - 34 -, - 36 -, - 37 -, - 40 -, - 42 -, - 45 -, - 46 -, - 49 -, - 59 -, - 60 -, - 73 -, - 84 -, - 97 -, - 99 -, - 104 -, - 105 -, - 108 -, - 114 -, - 115 -, - 154 -, - 192 -, - 202 -, - 204 -, - 206 -, - 215 -, - 217 -, - 219 -, - 221 -, - 222 -, - 224 -, - 226 -, - 227 -, - 238 -, - 249 -, - 250 -, - 254 -, - 260 -, - 284 -
office area - 73 -, - 84 -, - 99 -, - 104 -, - 108 -, - 180 -, - 204 -, - 227 -
office politics - 19 -
organisation - 100 -, - 179 -, - 200 -

P

perception - 159 -
performance - 102 -, - 133 -, - 148 -, - 159 -, - 197 -, - 199 -, - 200 -, - 201 -, - 204 -, - 245 -, - 262 -
performing - 73 -, - 80 -, - 81 -, - 200 -, - 201 -, - 245 -
plant - 35 -, - 45 -, - 143 -
positive change - 64 -, - 73 -
power - 26 -, - 55 -, - 87 -, - 122 -, - 147 -, - 195 -
presentation - 203 -, - 205 -, - 215 -, - 222 -, - 224 -, - 228 -
pressure - 19 -, - 23 -, - 55 -, - 115 -, - 205 -, - 217 -
procedure - 43 -, - 135 -, - 136 -, - 143 -, - 144 -, - 145 -, - 147 -, - 173 -, - 185 -, - 188 -, - 193 -
Procedures Manual - 129 -, - 135 -, - 143 -, - 146 -, - 147 -

process - 54 -, - 58 -, - 64 -, - 66 -, - 73 -, - 92 -, - 94 -, - 101 -, - 128 -, - 142 -, - 147 -, - 169 -, - 173 -, - 192 -, - 194 -, - 196 -, - 197 -, - 209 -, - 211 -, - 216 -, - 228 -, - 243 -
production - 40 -
productivity - 49 -
professional - 256 -, - 260 -
professionalism - 112 -
progress - 40 -, - 80 -, - 91 -, - 145 -, - 166 -, - 172 -
proposal - 214 -
protected conversation - 39 -, - 40 -
psychology - 71 -, - 169 -, - 261 -
purpose - 28 -, - 54 -, - 55 -, - 56 -, - 89 -, - 92 -, - 171 -, - 255 -, - 259 -

R

Recruitment - 193 -
regular - 47 -, - 50 -, - 54 -, - 55 -, - 56 -, - 72 -, - 95 -, - 121 -, - 124 -, - 142 -, - 172 -
relationship - 201 -, - 203 -, - 212 -, - 259 -, - 260 -
remove fear - 70 -, - 145 -
report - 64 -, - 67 -, - 74 -, - 106 -, - 120 -, - 128 -, - 135 -, - 143 -, - 172 -
reporting - 63 -, - 65 -, - 75 -, - 115 -, - 122 -, - 134 -, - 137 -
reputation - 28 -, - 191 -
responsibility - 102 -, - 108 -, - 118 -, - 122 -, - 123 -, - 127 -, - 139 -, - 149 -, - 159 -, - 185 -, - 187 -, - 210 -
results - 133 -, - 185 -, - 197 -, - 245 -, - 251 -, - 253 -
revenue - 34 -, - 40 -, - 106 -, - 115 -, - 116 -, - 185 -
rhythm - 47 -, - 49 -, - 54 -, - 147 -
Richard Koch - 262 -
role - 12 -, - 18 -, - 31 -, - 52 -, - 53 -, - 101 -, - 131 -, - 136 -, - 139 -, - 153 -
routine - 49 -, - 226 -
rules - 26 -, - 54 -, - 57 -, - 84 -, - 175 -

S

sales meetings - 20 -
salesteam - 34 -
scale - 179 -
self-respect - 204 -
set of principles - 252 -
Sir John Whitmore - 100 -, - 211 -
site - 98 -, - 214 -
solution - 95 -, - 106 -, - 147 -
staff - 21 -, - 22 -, - 35 -, - 43 -, - 47 -, - 60 -, - 71 -, - 96 -, - 98 -, - 99 -, - 115 -, - 127 -, - 157 -, - 159 -, - 171 -, - 193 -, - 195 -, - 205 -, - 206 -, - 218 -, - 226 -, - 259 -, - 262 -, - 283 -

start time	- 52 -, - 61 -
storming	- 73 -, - 74 -, - 80 -, - 81 -, - 146 -, - 183 -
structure	- 41 -, - 55 -
subconscious	- 177 -
success	- 16 -, - 17 -, - 67 -, - 172 -, - 201 -, - 245 -, - 282 -, - 283 -, - 295 -
support	- 36 -, - 99 -
synergy	- 49 -, - 88 -
system	- 78 -, - 79 -, - 116 -, - 128 -, - 134 -, - 136 -, - 191 -, - 192 -, - 193 -, - 197 -, - 250 -

---

T

take action	- 139 -
target	- 120 -, - 149 -, - 184 -, - 245 -
teaching	- 173 -
team	- 13 -, - 19 -, - 31 -, - 39 -, - 47 -, - 49 -, - 50 -, - 52 -, - 53 -, - 54 -, - 56 -, - 62 -, - 64 -, - 65 -, - 67 -, - 70 -, - 91 -, - 95 -, - 105 -, - 106 -, - 122 -, - 129 -, - 135 -, - 142 -, - 144 -, - 145 -, - 147 -, - 148 -, - 154 -, - 162 -, - 163 -, - 169 -, - 185 -, - 187 -, - 191 -, - 194 -, - 196 -, - 197 -, - 198 -, - 200 -, - 201 -, - 202 -, - 206 -, - 210 -, - 211 -, - 215 -, - 222 -, - 224 -, - 225 -, - 226 -, - 227 -, - 241 -, - 244 -, - 245 -, - 246 -, - 250 -, - 251 -, - 252 -, - 253 -, - 254 -, - 255 -, - 256 -, - 258 -, - 262 -, - 281 -, - 282 -, - 284 -, - 287 -
team coach	- 49 -
teamwork	- 19 -
techniques	- 71 -, - 95 -
terms	- 134 -, - 185 -, - 186 -
tests	- 258 -
Theory X	- 261 -
Theory Y	- 261 -, - 262 -
time	- 15 -, - 16 -, - 21 -, - 23 -, - 24 -, - 25 -, - 27 -, - 29 -, - 33 -, - 36 -, - 40 -, - 41 -, - 47 -, - 51 -, - 52 -, - 56 -, - 57 -, - 58 -, - 59 -, - 61 -, - 66 -, - 67 -, - 72 -, - 73 -, - 77 -, - 78 -, - 79 -, - 94 -, - 95 -, - 97 -, - 99 -, - 101 -, - 103 -, - 106 -, - 107 -, - 109 -, - 113 -, - 114 -, - 115 -, - 116 -, - 118 -, - 120 -, - 121 -, - 129 -, - 130 -, - 131 -, - 134 -, - 142 -, - 145 -, - 147 -, - 148 -, - 149 -, - 152 -, - 154 -, - 155 -, - 156 -, - 159 -, - 163 -, - 166 -, - 168 -, - 171 -, - 174 -, - 178 -, - 180 -, - 182 -, - 183 -, - 185 -, - 187 -, - 188 -, - 190 -, - 191 -, - 195 -, - 196 -, - 197 -, - 201 -, - 203 -, - 204 -, - 205 -, - 206 -, - 209 -, - 211 -, - 212 -, - 215 -, - 224 -, - 241 -, - 243 -, - 245 -, - 250 -, - 251 -, - 252 -, - 253 -, - 254 -, - 258 -, - 262 -, - 283 -, - 285 -, - 287 -
training	- 32 -, - 51 -, - 115 -
transparency	- 67 -, - 70 -, - 74 -, - 120 -
trust	- 47 -, - 257 -, - 258 -
Tuckman's Model	- 80 -
turnover	- 62 -, - 115 -

V

visualise — - 70 -

W

Who, What, When — - 78 -, - 109 -, - 122 -, - 129 -, - 135 -, - 243 -, - 250 -
work — - 16 -, - 21 -, - 28 -, - 31 -, - 34 -, - 40 -, - 41 -, - 42 -, - 43 -, - 47 -, - 48 -, - 53 -, - 56 -, - 67 -, - 74 -, - 80 -, - 88 -, - 92 -, - 94 -, - 98 -, - 107 -, - 115 -, - 123 -, - 133 -, - 135 -, - 136 -, - 137 -, - 139 -, - 144 -, - 152 -, - 163 -, - 166 -, - 169 -, - 170 -, - 192 -, - 193 -, - 194 -, - 200 -, - 201 -, - 202 -, - 212 -, - 214 -, - 215 -, - 221 -, - 224 -, - 226 -, - 241 -, - 249 -, - 260 -, - 281 -, - 282 -, - 283 -
workflow — - 40 -
workplace — - 151 -, - 163 -, - 252 -
workshop floor — - 34 -, - 35 -, - 95 -, - 96 -, - 98 -, - 107 -, - 108 -, - 117 -, - 122 -, - 174 -, - 226 -, - 240 -

Y

Yorkshire — - 16 -, - 285 -

ABOUT THE AUTHOR

Ian Kinnery is a world-class business coach and international speaker. He has more than thirty years' experience owning, managing and building businesses. He helps other business owners, leaders and leadership teams to perform at a much higher level than they dreamed possible. In particular, he helps them to scale up their businesses with minimum effort.

He holds professional awards for coaching and is a Rockefeller Habits Certified Scaling Up coach, Gallup Certified Strengths coach, a certified Emotional Intelligence coach, NLP master and an international speaker and presenter. He is widely revered as the 'team balance expert', as many testimonies of esteemed business leaders agree.

Printed in Great Britain
by Amazon